Bread and pastry recipes of the world famous chefs, United States, Canada, Europe; the bread and pastry book from the International cooking library - Primary Source Edition

A C. b. 1877 Hoff

Bread and Pastry Recipes

of the

WORLD FAMOUS CHEFS
United States
Canada
Europe

The Bread and Pastry Book

From the

INTERNATIONAL COOKING LIBRARY

Compiled and Edited by
A. C. HOFF

Los Angeles, Cal.
International Publishing Co.
1913

CONTRIBUTORS

Emile Bailly, Chef	Hotel St. Regis	New York City
Jean S. Berdou, Chef	Hotel Astor	New York City
Jean Millon, Chef	Ritz-Carlton	New York City
Henry Berger, Chef	Frankfurter-Hof	Frankfurt, Germany
Jules Kohler, Chef	Hotel Adlon	Berlin, Germany
G. Milhau, Chef	Tait-Zinkand Cafe	San Francisco
Adrian Delvaux, Chef	Hotel Baltimore	Kansas City
Otto Geutsch, Chef	Hotel Windsor	Montreal
Joseph D. Campazzi, Chef	Royal Poinciana	Palm Beach
E. C. Perault, Chef	Planters Hotel	St. Louis
John Chiappano, Chef	Auditorium Hotel	Chicago
Geo. R. Meyer, Chef	Rector's Cafe	Chicago
Gerard Embregts, Chef	Chateau Frontenac	Quebec
Louis Pfaff, Chef	New Willard Hotel	Washington
Henry Johannsen, Chef	Hotel Royal Palm	Miami
Victor Hirtzler, Chef	Hotel St. Francis	San Francisco
Emile Burgermeister, Chef	Hotel Fairmont	San Francisco
Martin Ginder, Chef	Hotel Green	Pasadena
Joseph Stoltz, Chef	Hotel Ponce de Leon	St. Augustine
Henri Boutroue, Chef	Hotel Shelbourne	Dublin, Ireland
Thos. Cooney, Chef	Van Nuys Hotel	Los Angeles
Jules Dauviller, Chef	Palace Hotel	San Francisco
Arthur Taylor, Chef	Hotel Raymond	Pasadena
Ernest Otzenberger, Chef	Hotel Dennis	Atlantic City
Cesar Obrecht, Chef	Grand Hotel de L'Europe	Lucerne, Switzerland
Jules Boucher, Chef	Arlington Hotel	Hot Springs
Chas. Grolimund, Chef	Washington Hotel	Seattle
Jean Juillard, Chef	Hotel Adolphus	Dallas
Chas. Pier Giorgi, Chef	Hotel Alcazar	St. Augustine
Peter Bona, Chef	Hotel Chamberlain	Fortress Monroe
Louis Lescarboura, Chef	Ft. Pitt Hotel	Pittsburgh
John Pfaff, Chef	Hotel Cape May	Cape May
Walter Jurenz, Chef	Hotel Galvez	Galveston
S. B. Pettengill, Chef	Hotel Ormond	Ormond Beach
Geo. E. Schaff, Chef	Hotel Albany	Denver
Ben E. Dupaquier, Chef	Hotel Arlington	Santa Barbara
William Leon Benzeni, Chef	Hotel Virginia	Long Beach
Chas. A. Frey, Chef	Hotel Alexandria	Los Angeles
Lucien Fusier, Chef	Grand Hotel Metropole	Interlaken, Switzerland
G. Cloux, Chef	U. S. Grant Hotel	San Diego
A. Schloettke, Chef	Westminster Hotel	Dresden, Germany
Lucien Raymond, Chef	Hotel Congress & Annex	Chicago
Louis Thein, Chef	Hotel Utah	Salt Lake City
Jules Edward Bole, Chef	Hotel Jefferson	St. Louis
John Bicochi, Chef	Hotel Piedmont	Atlanta
Edw. R. J. Fischel, Steward	Hotel Piedmont	Atlanta.
Leopold Saux, Steward	Hotel Grunewald	New Orleans
Henri D. Fouilloux, Steward	St. Charles Hotel	New Orleans

WORLD RENOWNED HOTELS

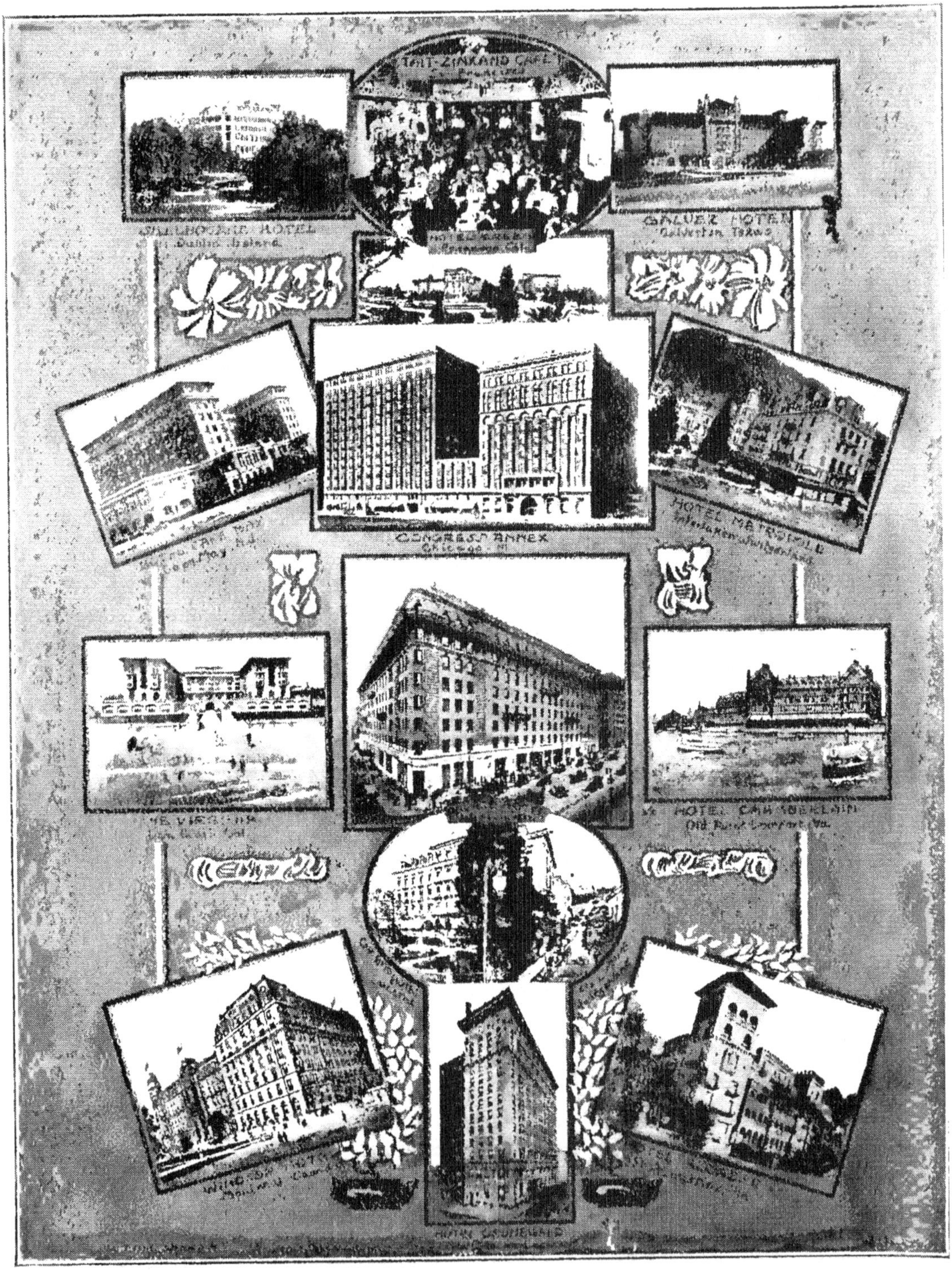

TAIT-ZINKAND CAFE

SHELBOURNE HOTEL
Dublin, Ireland

GALVEZ HOTEL
Galveston, Texas

CONGRESS ANNEX
Chicago, Ill.

HOTEL METROPOLE

HOTEL CHAMBERLAIN
Old Point Comfort, Va.

THEIR CHEFS-OUR CONTRIBUTORS

WORLD RENOWNED HOTELS

THEIR CHEFS-OUR CONTRIBUTORS

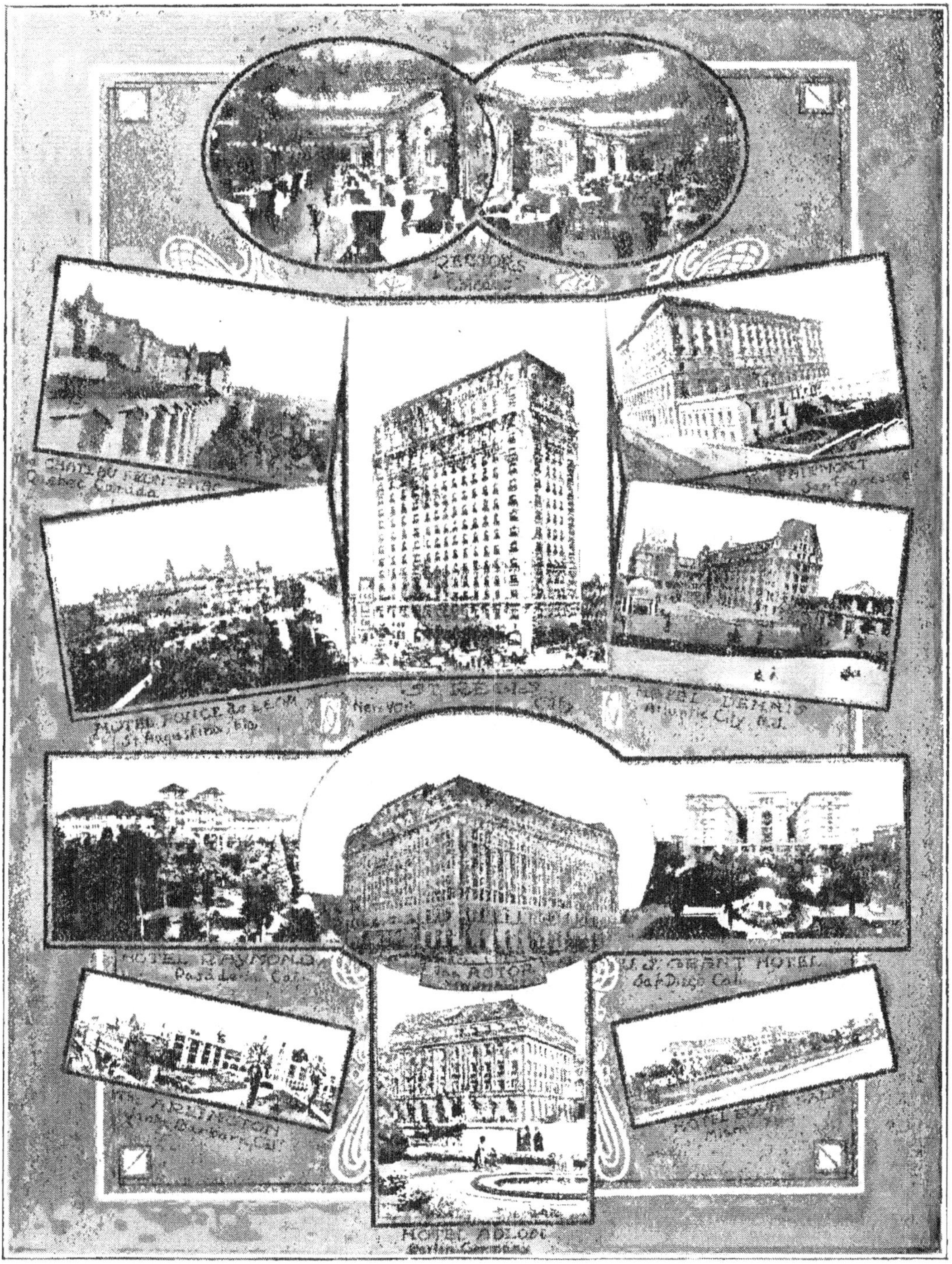

PREFACE

In presenting to the public this book on BREAD AND PASTRY RECIPES we feel that we are presenting the most complete authoritative and up-to-date book ever prepared on the subject. The contributors being the finest chefs in the United States, Canada and Europe insure every recipe shown as right. These world famous chefs have given us their special recipes and they have made the explanations so plain and so complete that any one can readily understand them.

The great chefs who have prepared these recipes for us have all made cooking their life work and have been apprenticed under the finest and most practical teachers in the culinary lines in this country and abroad.

A large portion of the copy has been translated from the French. The finest chefs are generally the French or Swiss. They are not literary men; their language is not flowery, but we know that even with the difficulty that exists in expressing in English many of the French terms that the work as a whole will be easily understood and greatly appreciated.

This is the first time in history that such a wonderful collection of recipes have been made obtainable for general use. These men are giving, in these recipes, their "professional secrets." The calibre of the men who have prepared these recipes is great and represents as much as the great masters in other lines of the world's work. Napoleon Bonaparte was a great general; Shakespeare, a great author; George Washington, a wonderful statesman; and Thomas Edison, a masterful inventor:—but we feel that the master chefs represented here are to be considered just as great and doing just as much of the world's work as any of the famous men we have all been taught to revere and respect.

The International Cooking Library, covering in ten volumes, every conceivable part, section or angle of the cooking question makes it possible for any one who will follow these recipes to be an expert cook. The great masters who have prepared these recipes have spent their

lives studying and experimenting and are giving in these recipes their best ideas and suggestions. These are dishes of the millionaires and the most particular epicureans.

We feel that this set of books is presented to the public at just the opportune time. All people are beginning to realize that there is really no more important art than cooking and this should be so; for what should be considered more important than what we eat? The best health insurance is having the right kind of foods, properly prepared. A man is at his best only when he is in robust health and nothing will undermine a person's constitution so quickly as poor food. The best dishes and the sure and absolute recipes for making them, are contained in this wonderful set of books. All the copy is from authorities just as positive and just as sure in this line as the noted Blackstone was on legal lines. We picked the best chefs in the world; we would accept copy from no others.

A careful study of the recipes and careful application of the directions for same is all that is necessary to produce the results that have made these men famous.

In the presentation of this book, we wish only that space would allow us to mention and pay courtesy to the many men who have assisted us in the various departments, copy preparation, translation, and editing, also the courtesies rendered by the managers of the world renowned hotels whose chefs have been our contributors.

INTERNATIONAL PUBLISHING COMPANY

INDEX

PASTRIES

WORLD RENOWNED HOTELS

PALACE HOTEL
San Francisco

FRANK BOCK
Pastry Chef

JULES DAUVILLER
Chef

FRANK BOCK
PASTRY CHEF
PALACE HOTEL
San Francisco, Cal.

Mr. Bock, prior to coming to the Palace, was with some of the best hotels in New York and Chicago as Pastry Chef. The Palace Hotel is noted for its Breads and Pastries.

Mr. Jules Dauviller, the Chef de Cuisine at the Palace Hotel, was formerly the $10,000 a year director of Cuisine in the home of Mr. and Mrs. Harry Payne Whitney, New York City. They got him from the Grand Hotel in Paris.

PRINCIPAL FACTS AND RULES ABOUT BREAD MAKING

To make bread is generally thought to be a very simple task, but it requires a thorough knowledge of the flours, as to their quality and strength; also of yeast as to its freshness. The climate, season, weather and temperature as well as the different degrees of baking heat needed for the various kinds of bread and rolls must be well studied, as they are factors to be considered; practice will teach these essential points. Bread being the staff of life, maintaining life longer than any other single food, should be made of the best materials to be healthful and strengthening. The superior qualities of this plain and simple food often induces people to overlook other shortcomings at meals. Establishments supplying a uniform, soft, sweet and fine grained delicious bread are known everywhere, for the superiority of their goods. Bakers encounter most difficulties from the varieties of flours in use. The east of this country produces flours of different qualities than the west. Good results only can be obtained by profound study of how to use them. Flours are classed as Winter wheat and Spring wheat. Winter wheats are divided into hard and soft red Winter wheat and soft white Winter Wheat. The soft grades are used for cake baking. Winter wheat flour excels in flavor and gives more moisture to the bread and also makes a larger and lighter loaf. Practical bakers use two and even three different brands of flour, from as many different mills.

Testing flour as to its strength may be made in taking of different flours the same quantities, mix them with the same quantity of water and the flour making the finest dough is the best. Another manner, but not as reliable can be made in pressing a small quantity of flour in the hand; if good it will retain its shape, coarse flour falls apart like sand.

Wheat flour should not be used, when freshly milled. Experienced bakers keep a certain supply of about six months' age on hand. The older the flour gets the whiter it will be and the better it will rise.

Western flours contain more starch than eastern flours. They are classed as weak flours but generally have a good flavor.

Graham flour consists of the entire grain ground up; the wheat should be good plump grain, but often is only bran mixed with second grade flours or ground corn. Graham flour should be bought from a reliable mill where only good wheat is used for the purpose.

Rye flour must be used freshly milled as in ageing it loses its flavor and strength. Corn meal, mostly in form of mush is also used in breads.

BREAD MAKING

Bread making is an operation divided in the preparation of the stock yeast, the ferment, the sponge, the dough, the moulding and the baking. In using compressed yeast, it saves time and labor. The manipulation is divided in only the sponge, the dough, the moulding and the baking. The exact quantity of flour and liquids to be used is very difficult to state as the variety of flours in the different parts of the country demands the judgment of the baker as to adding or decreasing the amount required.

In making doughs, especially the straight dough, the usual heat of the liquid must be lukewarm, from about seventy degrees to seventy-five degrees Fahrenheit. The flour should be kept in a warm dry place and also have the same temperature. In summer the straight dough may be mixed with ice water instead of warm. Fermentation sets in only some time after and the flour will become whiter, being longer in the dough state.

THE BAKE SHOP

The room or shop in which bread is made must be scrupulously clean, an evenly regulated temperature from about sixty to seventy degrees should prevail. This is obtained by heating or ventilating. Drafts injuring the raising of the dough must be prevented.

A steam chest is necessary in places where business on a larger scale is carried on. The goods can be raised in a shorter space of time. To save labor and time, troughs, benches, tables and other appliances, should be located in the handiest places.

Utensils for bread making are simple and few. An enameled castiron pot to cook potatoes, two tubs thirty inches deep and twenty inches in diameter, one for yeast, the other for ferment. A potato masher, a sieve to strain the hop water for stock, yeast and common yeast, a strainer for ferment, a sieve to sift flour, a dipper holding two quarts and a set of measures, to measure the liquids, casseroles to heat small quantities of liquids, also to melt lard or butter in. A wooden bowl for rubbing and mixing doughs like corn muffins; a pliable palette knife to scrape the dough from the sides of the bowl. A scraper, a strong iron plate with wooden handle fastened across the longest side of the plate, five inches wide and four inches long, for cutting and dividing the dough, also to scrape down the dough adhering to the sides of the trough. A bench brush and a dough brush, both long and flat about ten inches in length; a washbrush with handle ten inches in the whole length, handle to be five inches long to wash bread and rolls when taken out of the oven. Flat hair brushes, two inches wide, for greasing moulds and washing rolls, etc., with egg wash; a very thin, sharp plated knife, for making the incisions on bread and rolls; a pair of sharp and pointed scissors. Bread boxes measuring in the square thirty inches and four inches deep to raise the divided and moulded dough. Cloths, generally made of coarse linen, as sail cloth, to fit into this box, the length should be about twenty-five inches more, as they must be raised so as to support the bread or rolls which are baked on the hearth; one large rolling pin, made of hard wood with handles about three feet long and one inch and three-quarters in diameter. One or two smaller ones two feet long and five-eighths of an inch in diameter. Two hard wood boards, one ten inches long and four inches wide, the other twelve inches long and eight inches wide, very thin on one side and the other side half an inch thick on the long sides, to raise the bread from the boxes to the peel. Wooden peels with handles long enough to reach the farthest end of the oven, one with a plate twelve inches wide and thirty inches long for bread, the other fifteen inches wide and thirty-two inches long for rolls.

Russian sheet iron baking pans with sloping sides, bottom

twenty-two inches long by sixteen inches wide, top twenty-three inches long by seventeen and a half inches wide, height four inches for American loaves, containing six loaves of three pounds in weight.

Baking pans of Russian sheet iron with one and a half inch border, twenty-eight inches long by twenty inches wide, one side of the smaller ones must be without border.

Bread pans with hinged covers, sloping sides, for sandwich bread of four pounds measuring at the bottom, eighteen inches long and four inches wide, top eighteen and one-quarter inches long and five inches wide and four inches high. Instead of having covers, these pans can have a small hole in the bottom so when the loaves are placed in the pans they may be turned on baking sheets upside down, five loaves on one pan. Let them raise in the pan and ascertain the proof by inserting a straw through the hole. The pan should be filled to two-thirds.

Pans with sloping sides for graham and raisin bread, containing one pound and a half of bread dough, no covers, bottom seven and three-quarters of an inch long by four and a half inches wide. Top eight and one-quarter inches long by four and a half inches wide. Corn muffin pans of heavy tin twelve in a pan, muffin rings. A kneading trough made of hard wood with sloping front side, thirty inches wide at the top and twenty-two inches wide at the bottom; four to five feet long and twenty inches deep provided with a removable tight fitting cover, also a dividing board for the middle to hold the dough in desired space.

THE OVEN

Baking is the final and most important operation in bread making and may spoil the best of labor through carelessness. It is important to know how to heat an oven and ascertain the right heat required for the different kinds of bread and rolls as they demand various kinds of temperature. Ovens of every description are in use, the best ovens are the furnace brick ovens, they are heated in the baking chamber, with wood, coal, gas or oil and hold the heat well. Portable ovens are installed in many places. They are built on the principle and style of a furnace brick oven, are more light, less expensive and can be moved at any time; they are heated in the baking chamber. Shelf ovens are portable ovens which take up less space and are heated from beneath with any kind of fuel. The continuous patent furnace ovens are the best for large bakeries and hotels, being more practical as the firing is done under the baking chamber and baking can go on during the firing.

All of the bread and rolls baked in the hearth require ovens which hold steam and also must have tightly fitting doors and dampers; furthermore a steam tight oven is light. Vienna ovens as they are called, are built to hold steam and are built with a sloping hearth, so that the baking space is above the door, the steam will be retained when the door is opened. The other furnace ovens are supplied through steam pipes which should be placed in the back of the oven, as the steam coming from the back to the front will glace the bread more evenly and the steam will not escape as quickly when opening the door as by ovens which have steam pipes placed right in front above the door. Steam may also be generated by putting heavy sacks immersed in water in one of the back corners of the oven or by setting an iron pot with water in the fire place.

In portable ovens steam can be generated by putting a pan with water on the lower shelf. In most ovens the firing requires one hour's time, then the dampers and doors are shut and the oven laid off for one hour to distribute the heat evenly. After one hour's rest the oven is swabbed out. Continuous ovens are not laid off as baking can go on while the oven is heated. To ascertain the heat of the oven where no thermometer is attached to the oven, the test is made by throwing a handful of flour or cornmeal in the oven. When it blackens and burns the oven is too hot; if it slowly browns the oven has the right heat and baking can begin. Should the oven be too hot, it may rest longer and be swabbed out again, if too cold it must be fired again. Ovens with thermometers attached can be better regulated and once knowing the right degree a uniform hot oven can be had. Generally the pyrometer should register 550 degrees Fahrenheit, then the oven is shut down and when it registers 450 degrees Fahrenheit, it will be right for baking. As thermometers are placed often in the wrong places, it is necessary to find out the exact degrees needed through several trials. Once this knowledge is gained, it is an easy matter to always have the same heat required for the baking.

In some ovens the bottom heat will be too strong; swabbing out at different times will remedy this. In certain cases double pans must be used to prevent too much bottom color.

The rule for baking is to have all the bread and rolls which require the most heat ready first, and followed up with the goods which demand a lesser heat.

HOW TO MAKE YEAST

Stock Yeast

Boil five quarts of water, put five ounces of flour in a jar and make it into a firm paste with a part of the boiling water. To the remainder of the water add an ounce of hop, boil for ten minutes, remove from the fire and run through a fine sieve into the jar and over the paste. Set in a cool place until liquid is lukewarm. Dissolve the paste with the water and add four ounces of malt; cover and leave in a warm temperature for forty-eight hours without disturbing. After expiration of this time, strain this liquid in another stone jar. The stock yeast is now ready for use.

YEAST

Set fifteen quarts of water to boil in a good sized pot, remove it at the first boil from the fire. Put two pounds of flour in a tub and make with a pint of the boiling water a sufficiently hard paste. To the remaining water add three ounces of hops and boil for ten minutes; remove from fire and strain at once the boiling liquid through a fine sieve over the paste into the tub. Set in a cool place until lukewarm. Work the paste well into the water, using both hands; add right off one quart of stock yeast mixing all well together. Set the tub in a moderate temperature, do not disturb while fermentation takes place, which requires from eighteen to twenty hours. Strain this yeast through a fine sieve in another tub and set in an ice box or a very cool place. To be used as needed for the preparation of ferment. This yeast will keep for days if all details prescribed are carefully observed.

FERMENT

Wash seven quarts of small potatoes very clean; place in an enameled cast iron pot, cover with sufficient cold water, put on fire and let come to a boil; pour off this water and refresh with clean hot water and boil until well done. Throw the potatoes in a large tub and add two and one-half pounds of flour, mash well, to reduce to a smooth paste. Dilute this paste gradually with twenty-two quarts of cold or lukewarm water, observing temperature and season. Add five quarts of yeast and mix all well together. Set the tub in a moderately warm place and cover well with a cloth. Do not disturb until fermentation takes place, which means, when risen to the double of its height and falls again. Fermentation should take place in from seven to eight hours. This quantity is sufficient for one barrel of flour.

COMPRESSED YEAST

Compressed yeast being more uniform and reliable, is preferréd by most of the bakers and in places where only small quantities of bread are made it is more reliable, stronger and quicker than stock yeast and ferment, also not as quickly affected by change of weather; furthermore it is a saver of time and labor. Compressed yeast must be used as fresh as possible.

In parts of the country where yeast can not be had fresh daily, it is advisable to keep the yeast in a stone jar, well covered with water; in ice box. Change the water at least every second day, pouring it off carefully without disturbing the yeast. When using it pour off the water as directed and take out the required amount of yeast with a spoon, covering the remainder again with fresh cold water.

Common yeast or bakers ferment mixed with stock yeast is still used by a good many bakers, they claiming it makes a moister, sweeter and better loaf of bread than compressed yeast. For bakeries which must count the profits by making a larger quantity of bread of the same amount of flour, this yeast is mostly used and the sponge method prevails.

BREAD MADE OF SPONGE AND STRAIGHT DOUGH

Bread is made either by setting sponge and making dough afterwards or by making a straight dough. Bakers making a large sponge are enabled to make various kinds of doughs out of it and also save yeast. In setting sponge, dissolve the yeast well in the water and mix it with enough flour to make a soft dough. By using more or less yeast or colder or warmer water or making a softer or firmer sponge, in mixing more or less flour into it, the time of getting the sponge ready can be regulated. When sponge is ready, mix, dust over with flour, cover well and let rise. Sponge should be ready in four hours and it is, when bubbles begin to show which burst and throw off gas and the sponge flattens and drops in center. The sponge being ready, different doughs can be made in taking certain quantities of it and in adding the necessary ingredients for the different desired doughs as rolls, breads, coffee cakes, etc.

Sponge can be set cool at night and made into dough in the morning or can be set warm and slack with additional yeast to be taken after one hours time. Straight dough is made in mixing all ingredients at the same time, the use of more yeast is required than for sponge dough, according to temperature; by using more or less yeast it may be gotten ready in a few hours or to be worked up in the morning. Dough should be well mixed and kneaded; after it has risen, it should be worked over several times at different intervals.

Dough made of soft flour require a firmer dough than made of stronger flour, because dough slackens after it has been made. Strong flour can be made in a softer dough as it gives very little. The age of the dough depends on the strength of the flour and the firmness of the dough. A young dough colors more in baking and requires less heat than an old dough. Of the dough from which bread and rolls are made in the same time, bread should be made up first as it demands a younger dough than rolls, or a dough which has not raised too long.

FRENCH BREAD WITH FERMENT FOCKOS

Set a medium sponge with four quarts of ferment seventy-five degrees Fahrenheit to be ready in three hours. When ready to drop add one gallon of water seventy-five degrees Fahrenheit and six ounces of salt. Make a slack dough and beat it well, let rest for one hour. Divide up in one and a half pound pieces, mould round and put in slightly floured boxes; flatten them down to one-third of their thickness and dust over with flour, cover with another box air tight, let rise for about twenty to twenty-five minutes, mould them in long loaves. Set the loaves in cloth lined boxes dusted with flour and raise the cloth between each loaf to serve as support, so the dough in rising cannot flatten out. When set transfer to peel, wash over with water and make four or five slanting cuts with a very sharp thin plated knife. Put into the oven on the hearth. They should be baked in fifteen minutes; when baked, wash again with water.

FRENCH SPLIT LOAVES

Use a little firmer dough than for fockos. Make them up in the form of long Vienna shaped loaves and set them on boards. When they are moulded and slightly set, brush the top with lard and press each loaf lengthwise in the center with a long thin rolling pin, like split rolls. Arrange the loaves split side down in cloth lined boxes, raise the cloth between each for support and let rise. Sprinkle peel with a little white corn meal, turn split side up on a small board and transfer to peel and bake on the hearth without washing, to nice brown color.

MILK DOUGH

Different breads are made of part milk, others of all milk. When using nothing but milk, make a straight dough. The milk must be heated to the boiling point and cooled off to temperature required to season. When using milk and water, set the sponge with the water and add the milk when making the dough. When making straight dough, bring the milk to a boil and add the water; let cool down to desired temperature about seventy-five degrees Fahrenheit. All milk breads take more color while baking and therefore demand a lower heat, also less time to rise.

HOME MADE BREAD

Make a medium straight dough from one gallon water, half milk. Heat the milk to boiling point and add the water, cool down to seventy degrees Fahrenheit. Dissolve four ounces yeast in this liquid, add three and a half ounces of salt, four ounces of sugar and two ounces of butter or lard. Mix all ingredients up well with the water and milk and make the dough with a good strong wheat flour. Let set, dough should be ready in two hours; when raised to the double of its original size, fold it over from all four sides and press down. Let rise again for about three-quarters of an hour, fold over again, divide into pieces, mould round and put in boxes to set for about twenty minutes and make them into loaves, pressing two opposite sides together with the palms of the hand. Lay in the moulds smooth

side up and set to rise until the pan is almost full. Bake and brush over with a wash of white of egg and water well beaten together. Mould should be, when filled, about half full. From the same dough, when made in a larger quantity, you can make Vienna loaves of two pounds of dough each, sandwich loaves in single loaves or made up in American loaf style.

For Vienna loaves mould the two pound pieces round, let rise twenty minutes and form long loaves from them, manipulating as prescribed for pan loaves. These loaves are arranged in cloth lined wooden boxes with the smooth side down and the cloth raised between each loaf as support. When sufficiently set, transfer to peel, smooth side up, with the aid of the board as mentioned in utensils; wash over with water when no steam is applied and bake on the hearth to a nice brown color. When baked and taken out of the oven, wash with white of egg. For sandwich loaves, scale off four pound pieces, mould round and put in pans, after having formed the loaves from them, either in the bread pans with hinged covers or in the pans with the hole in the center of the bottom of the pan; the latter are turned up side down on a baking sheet about four to five loaves on one pan, as soon as the mold is fitted. Bake in steam. American loaves are scaled to three pound pieces, molded as the others, but arranged side by side in the baking sheet iron pan. For this purpose the sides of the loaves may be slightly greased with melted lard to obtain a smooth and even break when baked. Let set to almost double of its original size and bake in a medium hot oven, without washing. All these pan baked breads, without exception must be turned out of the moulds as soon as baked.

HOME BREAD WITH WATER ONLY

Make a straight dough at seventy-five degrees Fahrenheit from one gallon of water, three ounces of sugar and three ounces of lard or butter, with a good strong flour. This dough should be ready raised in four hours or it will flatten out and lose its resistance. Must be worked over well and rise again for twenty minutes; scale mould and form in loaves for pans. Let these loaves set to about two-thirds the height of the pan and bake.

VIENNA BREAD MADE OF STRAIGHT DOUGH

Make a very firm dough of three quarts of water and one quart of milk, about eighty degrees fahrenheit, two ounces of yeast, three ounces of salt, six ounces of sugar and six ounces of lard or butter or half butter and half lard. This dough should rise and be ready in four hours, work it down again by folding it over from the four opposite sides and pressing it down. Cover and let come up again; when set, work it over once more; let rise another time and scale in two pound pieces, mould round and in twenty to twenty-five minutes after form in oblong pointed loaves as prescribed before. Put in cloth lined boxes smooth side down, raise cloth between as usual. When set put on peel sprinkled over with a little flour, butter or white corn meal. By the aid of a thin board, from there transfer to peel by sliding it on its smooth side up. Should be baked with steam; when no steam can be generated, wash over with water and give three slanting cuts, bake on hearth. When baked, wash over with a thin white of egg wash.

When baking in a range the loaves may be put on slightly greased baking sheets washed over with a thin egg wash made out of a whole egg and milk.

VIENNA BREAD MADE OF SPONGE

Make a slack sponge with two ounces of yeast, one gallon of water seventy-five degrees Fahrenheit; work it well, sprinkle with flour and cover. When the sponge is ripe and has fallen in the center add the milk the same temperature as the water, also three ounces of salt, four ounces of sugar and four of lard or butter. Work all these ingredients well into the dough and make a firm dough with good strong flour. Let the dough rise to double of its size and working well down again let it come up again and divide in equal pieces of one and a half pounds or more. Mould into balls, let set again for twenty minutes and shape long loaves with pointed ends out of these balls; put in cloth lined boxes as mentioned in the former recipes and bake in steam or on the hearth.

PULLMAN BREAD

For Pullman bread use any good milk dough which is not too stiff. It should be passed several times through rollers which are fastened to the bench or table with clamps, before moulding into loaves. It is used mostly for sandwiches especially in railroad stations and dining cars. The pans in which this bread is baked should be ten inches long, four and a half inches wide and four inches high with a sliding cover. Give three-quarters proof in the pan, close the cover and bake in a medium hot oven. Breads baked in covered pans have the advantage to retain their moisture longer, have a better taste and the crust is very thin. The waste will also be minimized, when these loaves are cut for sandwiches.

RAISIN BREAD

Make a rather stiff dough of one gallon sweet milk, boil the milk first and cool down to seventy degrees Fahrenheit; add six ounces of yeast, four ounces of salt, twelve ounces of sugar, sixteen ounces butter and eight eggs. Mix all these ingredients well with the milk, and make with a strong flour a straight dough. Cover and let rise for two hours. After it has raised double its size, work one and a half pounds Sultana raisins and one and a half pounds of currants in the dough. Scale into one and a half pound loaves, let rise for twenty minutes, form the loaves and put in pans. Pan should be half full. Let prove to three-quarters of the height of the pan and bake in medium hot oven.

NEW ENGLAND BREAD NO. ONE

Make a firm straight dough of one gallon of water and half a can condensed milk seventy-five degrees Fahrenheit, two ounces of salt and three ounces sugar. When set work it down again; let rise for fifteen minutes, scale and work into loaves, bake in moulds in good oven.

NEW ENGLAND BREAD NO. TWO

Make of twenty ounces corn meal, a mush to begin with. Make a straight dough at seventy-five degrees Fahrenheit from two gallons water, six ounces yeast, six ounces salt, six ounces sugar, six ounces of lard and the corn meal mush. Mix all ingredients thoroughly with the water before adding the flour. Cover and let rise for four hours, work it well after this time has elapsed and let come up again for about twenty-five minutes. Mould in loaves, manipulating like other breads; let rise to two-thirds of its height of pan and bake in a good heat.

HOME MADE BREAD WITH FERMENT

Make a straight dough with three quarts ferment, one quart of water or milk and five ounces of salt at a temperature of about eighty degrees. Work the dough well and pen it close up in the trough, let come up and work over, let raise about half. Throw the dough on the table, divide, mould round, put in the box and after it sets for ten minutes, form in loaves. Bake in a good heat.

GRAHAM BREAD NO. ONE

Make a medium straight dough of one gallon of water, five ounces of yeast, four ounces of salt, three ounces lard and one pint of molasses. Mix these ingredients well; add four pounds of good graham flour and the rest of a good strong wheat flour. Let rise about two hours and work it down again. Throw on table, mold up as other breads in one and a half pound loaves, set in pans and let rise in the moulds to two-thirds of their height, bake in medium hot oven.

GRAHAM BREAD NO. TWO

Make a rather soft straight dough of one gallon of water, one and a half ounces yeast, three ounces salt, four ounces lard and three-quarters of a pint of molasses. Use half graham and half wheat flour. Let come up but once, work it down again, let rise for a few minutes; scale and mould into pans, set to rise, bake in medium hot oven. This dough has to be made cool and must be worked up young. This means don't give much proof.

GLUTEN BREAD

Gluten bread can be made of water or partly milk and is treated like graham bread. For six persons, the sweetening and shortening is omitted. Make a straight dough of two quarts of water and two quarts of milk, one and a half ounces of yeast, three ounces salt, six ounces lard and half a pint molasses. Use only gluten flour to make the dough and let come up only once. Work down and after a short interval, proceed moulding in loaves as usual and bake in a medium hot oven.

RYE BREAD

Make a rather stiff straight dough of seventy degrees Fahrenheit from one gallon of water, three ounces of yeast and five ounces of salt. Use a fresh well flavored rye flour mixed with the same quantity of a second grade wheat flour. Let come up once; work down and let set about ten minutes; divide in two pound pieces and mould round. When all are formed, shape right off in long, round pointed loaves, pressing the seam well together. Place on boards or in boxes covered with cloth, smooth sides down, raise cloth for support and let come only one-third its size. Turn on with corn meal or rye flour dusted peel, wash over with water, give three or four slanting cuts across and bake in a hot oven. Wash again with a thin white of egg; wash again as soon as taken from the oven. May also be baked in well greased pans which is more handy for the housewife.

GERMAN RYE BREAD

German rye bread is made of a part of sour rye dough. To start this sour dough, take three pounds of yeast raised rye dough. Dissolve in one quart of water and mix with enough rye flour to make a very slack dough. Let this sponge stand until the next day and use it in adding some compressed yeast for the first rye bread dough. Keep every day a piece of this dough to make the next day's bread. From one gallon of water, one pound of sour dough, one ounce yeast, three ounces salt and some caraway seeds, make a very firm dough, using two-thirds of rye flour and one-third of wheat flour. Dissolve the yeast and sour dough well in the water before adding salt, seed and flour. Work it well and let rise about double its size; work over again and make up in round or long loaves. Set these loaves on thickly dusted boards, using half cornmeal and flour. Let prove only to one-third its original size and bake on hearth in a hot oven. These loaves during setting must be washed over with water from time to time and before baking make some round holes with a stick or give slanting cuts. Do not set the loaves too close together in the oven until baked well, then they can be moved close together while finishing the baking.

HALF RYE BREAD

Set a sponge with two quarts of water, one ounce of yeast and wheat flour. When ready, add two quarts of water, three ounces of yeast, also some caraway seed and make a medium dough with two parts of rye flour and one part of wheat flour. Let set, work down and when ready make long loaves, the shape of Vienna bread. Set in cloth lined boxes with smooth sides down; raise the cloth between each. Let rise to two-thirds its size and bake in hot oven, washing and cutting them before baking. When baked, wash over again either with water or a thin corn starch paste or white of egg mixed and well beaten with water.

BOSTON BROWN BREAD

Two pounds of corn meal, two pounds of graham flour, two pounds rye flour, two pounds of wheat flour, one quart boiling water, one quart molasses, two ounces of salt, three ounces yeast. Scald the cornmeal first, by pouring the boiling water on and stirring it, add the molasses and salt. When only lukewarm, add the yeast, then mix in the graham, rye and wheat flour. The dough should be like graham dough, when too stiff, soften with milk. After a little kneading on the table, grease the pan in which it was mixed, place the dough in it, cover well with a cloth and let rise for about six hours in moderate temperatured place. When ready throw on table, knead again a little and make in five loaves. Place in high round moulds, made especially for brown bread, let rise for half an hour, put the tight fitting covers on and steam in a steam chest about four hours and bake for twenty minutes. If no steamer can be used, the bread can be baked in a cool oven, registering about 250 degrees Fahrenheit, proceed as follows: Set the pails into a pan with high borders containing from two to three inches of water, push into oven carefully and bake for five hours.

BOSTON BROAD BREAD WITH SODA OR BAKING POWDER

One pound graham flour, one pound of rye flour, two pounds of corn meal, one pound wheat flour, one quart molasses, three pints of milk, two ounces salt, one ounce of baking soda, or instead of soda, three ounces of baking powder. Mix all the flours together, dissolve the soda in the milk, add the salt and molasses and make a soft dough, add more milk if required. Fill the Boston brown bread pails, three-quarters full. Steam for three hours and bake fifteen minutes. Covers of pails must be tight fitting. When using baking powder, mix the powder well with the flours.

BOSTON BROWN BREAD WITH FERMENT

Put into a bowl or pan, two and three-quarter pounds of yellow corn meal, two pounds of white corn meal, one pound and three-quarters of rye flour, one pound of Boston meal, one ounce of salt. Dilute these flours with one quart molasses, one quart ferment and two quarts of water. Add the salt and make a very slack paste, mixing all well together. Cover and leave to rise in a moderate temperature for four hours. Add after this interval, three-quarters of an ounce of soda dissolved in a glassful of water and twelve ounces of bread crumbs. Mix all well together. Fill this paste in buttered brown bread pails about two-thirds full, let stand for one hour. Cover with lid and bake in a very slow oven six hours. Put the moulds in high rimmed pans containing two inches of water.

PULLED BREAD PALACE

Of freshly baked milk bread either baked in pans with sliding cover or in the American loaf style; take off the crusts and pull either with the aid of two forks or breaking the loaf in three parts and using your hand; long strips, they may have any shape, toast on baking sheets in a medium oven to a nice brown. Bread must be turned once or twice to have a uniform color on all sides. When oven is too hot, the inside will not be crisp. Served with almost every meal on the same plate as rolls. Very healthy, especially for invalids.

BOSTON CREAM TOAST

While toasting the bread, bring a sufficient quantity of milk to a boil and thicken with cornstarch, dissolve in a dish and cover with creamy milk preparation.

FRENCH TOAST (One Portion)

Three slices bread, trim off the crusts, cut in triangle shape and saturate with a preparation of one beaten egg, three teaspoonfuls of sugar and a little milk or if wanted richer, with cream instead of milk. Fry in a shallow pan in clarified butter to a golden brown. As soon as done dust sugar over them and serve very hot.

MELBA TOAST

Cut bread slices of which the crust is trimmed in diamond shape and toast instead of on the griddle, on a baking pan in the oven, to a nice brown color on both sides. When done sift sugar over them and serve at once.

DIFFERENT TOASTS GARNISHED

TOASTS, GARNISHED WITH CHICKEN

Bacon, chopped chicken, lettuce, caviar, foie-gras, anchovies, sardines, roast beef and horseradish, hot roast beef with gravy, broiled sardines, chicken and green peppers.

Toast slices of bread on both sides, and let cool, butter with mustard or anchovy butter on the buttered side, lay desired garnishing and serve.

TOAST WITH OLIVE OIL AND CHEESE

Dip some toast in olive oil and arrange them on a dish; strew over some grated parmesan cheese, pepper and lemon juice. Put them for a few minutes in the oven to give just enough time for the cheese to melt and serve as soon as they leave the oven.

SARDINE TOAST WITH OLIVE OIL

Instead of the cheese, pound a few anchovies with an equal quantity of butter and a little parsley. Cover the toast with this butter. Of a few sardines wipe off the skins with a cloth, arrange on top of the toast, put in the oven for a few minutes and serve hot.

FANCY SANDWICHES FOR AFTERNOON TEAS

The bread for sandwiches, should be cut as thin as possible from loaves baked in covered pans. Bread one day old or even a little older will answer the purpose better, because it does not crumb in the cutting as fresh bread does. When sandwiches are ready and cannot be served right away, they must be folded in slightly wetted napkins to keep fresh. The butters used for sandwiches are generally, mustard, butter, anchovy butter and foie-gras butter.

Mustard butter is butter mixed well with salt, red pepper and mustard. For anchovy butter, add a little essence of anchovy to it; for foie-gras butter, take same quantity of butter as foie-gras pound them well together and press through a sieve.

Anchovy butter may also be made of one ounce of anchovies. Wipe the skins off well with a cloth to remove all the scales, pound little cayenne pepper and rub through a sieve.

When meats and poultry are used, spread mustard butter on the bread. For game, use foie-gras butter, and anchovy butter for fish. There is no regular rule as to the exact use of these butters, and each one can follow their own taste and fancy.

BARLOW SANDWICHES

Butter the bread slices with mustard butter. Some pickled cucumbers, and on these some finely shredded and seasoned lettuce hearts; on top of this, slices of chicken, the same size as bread, cut very thin; then some more lettuce hearts and finely chopped hard boiled eggs over all, cover with another bread slice. Cut any shape desired and serve on dishes covered with folded napkins.

SCRAPED CHICKEN SANDWICH

Scrape white chicken meat very fine with the aid of a fork, season, salt and pepper, spread over the bread, English mustard butter, cover with another slice of buttered bread, trim off the crust and cut in diamond shape.

SLICED CHICKEN AND LETTUCE

Slice the white chicken meat very thin, arrange nicely on mustard butter covered bread slices. On top of meat place the leaves of the heart of lettuce salad, cover with well flavored mayonnaise and cover with another slice of bread; trim and cut in triangle or diamond shapes.

SHREDDED CHICKEN

Cut the white chicken meat, julienne style, which means in very fine strips the thickness of one-eighth of an inch and in lengths half to three-quarters of an inch. Mix with a mustard mayonnaise just enough to bind the meat; spread on bread slices, not buttered and roll up like a jelly roll. Tie with very narrow blue and red fancy ribbon.

CHICKEN SALAD PALACE

Cut the chicken meat and the celery in very small dice; mix with mayonnaise and spread on buttered bread. Cut in small squares.

TURKEY AND TONGUE

Cut the white meat of turkey very thin, also the tongue. Arrange slices of both on mustard buttered slices of bread. Cover and trim; cut in square or diamond shape.

TURKEY

Cut turkey meat very thin; cover mustard buttered bread slices with it and cut in squares or triangle shape. Tongue and ham sandwiches are prepared in the same manner.

TURKEY, HAM AND TONGUE

These sandwiches can also be made of the meats and butter passed through the machine to make a smooth paste from them. Spread the different meat pastes on bread slices and cover. Cut in any shape desired when trimmed off.

SALAMI

Must be cut very thin and arranged on mustard buttered bread slices.

PRESSED BEEF

Cut the beef very thin and proceed as for other sandwiches as chicken, etc.

TOMATO

Slice the tomatoes very fine, put on mustard buttered bread slices.

SWISS CHEESE

Cut Swiss cheese very thin and finish as the preceding.

WATER CRESS

Cut the leaves from the stems and put on the buttered bread slices.

NEUFCHATEL CHEESE

Mix the cheese with finely chopped chives and season with paprika.

LETTUCE

Chop the hearts of lettuce fine and mix with mayonnaise: proceed as before mentioned.

EGG

Spread over the bread mayonnaise and cut hard boiled eggs in slices and sprinkle finely chopped fine herbs over the eggs. Fine herbs consist of parsley, chervil, tarragon and chives.

PIMENTOES

Mustard buttered bread slices with fine sliced pimentoes on top.

ANCHOVIES

Spread mustard butter over the bread and arrange fillets of anchovies on top. Cut in squares or triangles.

ANCHOVY PASTE

Spread this paste over the mustard buttered bread. Anchovy as well as regalia-fish pastes are sold in all first class groceries.

REGALIA FISH PASTE

When using this paste add a little Worcestershire sauce for seasoning. Same proceeding as anchovy.

PATE DE-FOIE-GRAS

Pound the same quantity of butter as foie-gras well together; press through a sieve and spread over the bread.

NUTS AND OLIVES

Hack the nuts very fine and mix with mayonnaise. All kinds of nuts may be used. Olives hacked fine and bound with mayonnaise.

CAVIAR

Spread bread over with mustard butter and a layer of Caviar on top. Cut desired shape, serve with these sandwiches on nice leaves of lettuce, arrange nicely on separate dish, one leaf with the finely chopped yellow of the eggs, one leaf with very finely cut onions and one leaf with finely cut up chives. Serve also lemons or limes, cut either in half or quarter pieces.

GAME SANDWICHES

Spread the bread over with foie-gras butter. Lay some thinly sliced or chopped up game on top, cover with another slice of foie-gras buttered bread, press down, trim nicely and cut in desired shapes.

BREAKFAST ROLLS

Make a rather stiff dough from one gallon lukewarm milk, six ounces of yeast, four ounces of salt, three-quarters of a pound of sugar, eight eggs and one pound of butter with a strong wheat flour. Before adding the flour, all of the ingredients must be exceedingly well mixed with the milk. Dust a little flour over the dough, cover well and leave to rise; it should be ready in two hours and double its volume. When at this stage fold the dough over from the four sides and press it down. Let come up for about twenty-five minutes. Scale off in three and a half pound pieces, roll out in long round sticks, divide these in thirty-six equal parts; one weighing about one and a half ounces. Mould in round balls, dust flour over them and let set ten minutes and form into different shaped rolls as, round, oblong with pointed ends with four incisions forming a cross; pocket book shape, split, crescents. Some of these may be bestrewn with poppy seeds.

All round, as soon as the balls are moulded in a more symmetrical round form, place on greased baking sheets with a little space between each other, to give enough room to rise. When they are two-thirds their original size, wash them with a thin egg wash and bake.

Oblong, with pointed ends; roll the balls oblong and on both ends very thin.

Round with cross on top; the same proceeding as for round; cut when raised and washed over. Cut four deep incisions with the scissors so as to form a cross.

Pocket book, lay two rolls alongside of each other with enough room between so as they do not touch each other. With a very thin rolling, press them down in the center and roll a little depression in center, butter the both thicker sides with melted butter and fold them over like a book, press them down a little on the back and set on baking sheets with enough space so that they do not touch each other. Before baking wash with a thin egg wash.

Split: place two balls as told before along side of each other; grease in the center with melted lard or butter and press lengthwise across the center; let both sides come together and place on baking sheets like the rest.

Crescents: take two of the balls and place side by side a little distance apart and with a thin rolling, about the thickness of a broom handle, roll out to an oval size and an eighth of an inch thick, leaving the two farthest sides a little thicker, than the forward ones. Then with the left hand hold the front part of the farthest end by rolling it over on itself to bring it to the forward end, to give it the shape of a shuttle six inches long, one inch thick in the center and one-fourth of an inch on both ends. When finished, lay them on slightly greased baking sheets giving them the shape of a crescent. Let rise and brush over with an egg wash made of beaten egg and milk. Bake in a slow oven for about fifteen minutes. Different of these rolls as the round split and crescent shapes can be washed and dipped in poppyseed as soon as they are made up and before putting them on the baking sheets. Out of the same dough other shapes may also be formed.

DOUGH FOR SMALL ROLLS AND FINGER ROLLS

Make a small sponge of half an ounce of yeast and one-quarter of a pound of flour with a little warm water. Place in a vessel and let rise in a temperate place to the double of its size. Weigh three-quarters of a pound of flour on the table, make a hollow in the center, in this put a pinch of salt, half an ounce of sugar and a little tepid milk, also two eggs. Mix the flour gradually into these ingredients and add the rest of the lukewarm water which should measure three-quarters of a gill. When all are mixed knead the paste well, beating it on the table to incorporate as much air as possible. As soon as the paste has plenty of body, knead one ounce of butter well into it, then add another ounce of butter and knead the paste well for a few minutes longer. At last mix the sponge lightly into the dough, put back into the bowl, cover and leave to rise again in a moderately warm place. When the dough is raised, divide into one-pound pieces, roll them out into long round strips, half an inch in diameter. Divide these rolls into twenty equal sized pieces, mold in round balls with the palm of the hand. Let these balls set a little and shape in small rolls with pointed ends two and three-quarters of an inch long. Arrange them not too closely on a slightly greased baking sheet and let rise. When sufficiently raised, brush them over twice with egg wash, and bake in a warm oven.

FINGER ROLLS

Sift two pounds of flour on the table; take half a pound of this flour, make a hollow in the center and in this put one ounce and a half of yeast; dissolve with a gill and a half of lukewarm water and make a soft sponge with the flour. Mold a round ball from it, cut a cross on the top and place in casserole containing lukewarm water; cover and let rise about fifteen minutes to double its size. Form a circle with the rest of the flour and put in the center of it two ounces of sugar, half an ounce of salt, two eggs and two and a half gills of barely lukewarm water. Mix ingredients well together and make a consistent dough with the flour. Knead it well a few minutes on the table until it acquires body, incorporate two ounces of butter and knead until smooth. When the sponge is ready mix it well with the dough, put it in a bowl, cover and let rise in a moderate temperature for one hour. When raised to double its size, press down again, and divide into half pound pieces; divide these into twelve equal sized parts, mold them round and let rise about fifteen minutes. Roll out in four and a half inch long round sticks, arrange them on greased baking pans, not too near together, about a quarter of an inch apart, put to rise to one-third the original size, brush over with a light egg wash and bake in a hot oven.

MILK ROLLS

Make a straight firm dough from one gallon of lukewarm water, milk, four ounces of yeast, three ounces of salt and four ounces of sugar, let set to double its size; knead down and throw on table. Scale off in three and a half pound pieces, divide these in thirty-six equal parts, roll up in balls, dust over with flour and let come on for a few minutes. Make split rolls of half the balls as prescribed for sweet rolls, set on baking sheets, let rise and bake, washing them over with water before and after baking. They may also be washed with a very thin beaten egg wash. Knead half of the balls, roll out into long round sticks about four and a half inches long. Arrange on baking sheets and brush over before putting them in the oven, with egg wash. Bake in a medium hot oven.

WATER ROLLS (Sponge Method)

Make a slack sponge of three quarts lukewarm water and three ounces of yeast; let this sponge ripen; it should be ready in four hours. When it flattens and falls in center, showing bubbles which burst and throw off gas, add three quarts of water the same temperature as before, two ounces sugar and six ounces salt. Mix these well with the sponge and make a medium stiff dough with a good wheat flour. Let rise to double its size. Throw it out on the table and fold over from all sides, pressing it down; divide in two ounce pieces, mould them round and arrange on a slightly flour dusted board. When they have set ten minutes, grease in the center with a little melted lard and press one by one well lengthwise in the middle with a very thin rolling pin. Replace on board, split side downwards. When set sufficiently, put them on the peel in rows and arrange so as not to touch each other while baking. Wash over and put on hearth. Bake in steam in hot oven.

VIENNA ROLLS (Sponge)

Set a stiff sponge of four quarts lukewarm water, two ounces yeast in summer and three ounces yeast in winter, with a strong wheat flour, dust over with flour and let set. When the sponge has fallen for the first time in the center, add two quarts of lukewarm milk, half a pound of sugar, three and a half ounces of salt, six ounces of lard and six ounces of butter; instead of butter, specially prepared tasteless cotton seed oil may be used, about one dipper containing two quarts. Incorporate all ingredients well into the sponge and make a rather stiff dough, working it in small pieces several times over, which lay on top of each other. Let set to double its volume; throw the dough on the bench and fold over; let come up again and press down another time. Divide in one and a half ounce pieces; mould round and arrange in flour dusted boxes, dusting them over with flour. After fifteen minutes, you can make up different kinds of rolls as kaisersemmel, weckerl, crescents, salt sticks, twists and other shapes.

Kaisersemmels are folded four times; perfect rolls of this kind can only be made by long practice. The manipulation is as follows: Flatten a previously moulded round piece of dough with your right hand; take hold of one end of the dough with your left hand, holding the thumb on top, supporting the bottom with the other fingers. Fold a small part of dough over the thumb as to form a hole and press it with the side of the left hand, down in the center to stick. Fold over another part also pressing it next to the first in center; repeat this four times. The last time stretch the remaining outer end to a point and press well into the hole, removing the thumb, which must be kept in the same position during the entire operation. Place on flour dusted boards or cloth lined boxes, some distance apart with folded side down; let rise to two-thirds its size, turn on peel folded side up. Cover with water and bake in medium hot oven in steam on the hearth.

Weckerl, the same proceeding as mentioned for water rolls, split side down while setting and split side up when baking.

Crescents are treated the same way as told in recipe for breakfast rolls. They are placed in boxes set and baked on the hearth. Poppy seed may be used and this seed must be put on before setting to proof, washing the crescents over and dipping them in the seed. The side with the seed is turned upwards.

Salt sticks are rolled like crescents in shape of a shuttle. They are washed and dipped in a mixture of salt and caraway seed. Arrange on boards, salt covered side upwards; when set, bake like the others in steam.

Twists: divide the round moulded pieces into three equal parts each, roll them out long, with pointed ends all the same length. Lay three of these long pointed rolls, side by side and braid them, beginning in the middle and turning them over on the other side and finish braiding. Both pointed ends must be well closed by pressing them together. Use poppy seed and clip them like salt sticks.

All of these different kinds of rolls are baked on the hearth in a medium hot oven and in steam. They must be so arranged all ready on the peel, that they do not touch each other while baking.

GERMAN ROLLS

From one gallon of milk, eight ounces of yeast and two and a half ounces of salt, make a slack straight dough with good strong flour. Dust over with flour, cover and put in a temperate place to set for half an hour. Throw it then on the table, dust well with the flour and work it in small portions, not over one pound; replace in the same manner. Divide them in two ounce pieces and mould in long oval shape. Arrange in cloth lined boxes to set; transfer to peel, make a deep cut across the roll and bake in a medium oven on the hearth and in steam. If steam is not available, wash over with water before baking and again with a thin cornstarch when they come out of the oven.

PARKER HOUSE ROLLS

Make a rather stiff dough from one gallon of milk, four ounces of yeast, six ounces of sugar, two ounces of salt, twelve ounces of butter and a good strong wheat flour; set to raise and when the dough is ready divide in one and a half ounce pieces and mould them round. When proved a little, press them down in center and roll out about three-quarters of an inch in the center. Brush both thick sides over with a little melted lard and fold them together; press the thin outer back part down with the side of the hand. Arrange them on a greased baking sheet close enough to touch each other or if desired, farther apart to make single rolls. Give only one-third proof and wash before baking. If proofed in steam chest, they need no washing but should be brushed over with butter when baked.

SANDWICH ROLLS

Make a straight dough from one gallon water, two ounces of yeast, one pound lard, two ounces salt, ten ounces sugar, and good wheat flour. Let raise and work down again. Divide in two ounce pieces. Mould them round and arrange on greased pans, so they do not touch each other. Let set double its size and bake in a hot oven; wash before baking. Instead of round they may be made up in oblong shape.

GRAHAM ROLLS

Make in a bowl a medium straight dough of four pounds of good graham flour, the rest strong wheat flour and one gallon of water; one pint molasses, four ounces salt, five ounces of yeast and three ounces of lard. Set to raise, when raised double its volume, fold over and press down. Throw the dough out on the table and divide in one and a half ounce pieces; mould them either round or oval shape, set on pans, give medium proof, and bake in a good heat. After baking, brush over with an egg wash of whites of eggs and water.

GRAHAM GEMS

Make a slack dough as follows: Sift one pound of wheat flour and three ounces of baking powder together. Put this flour in a bowl and add three pounds of unsifted graham flour; mix both well together and make a hollow in center. Place in this hollow, three ounces of molasses, two ounces melted lard and one ounce of salt. Add milk or water to make a soft mixture and rub smooth; fill in greased muffin pans and bake in a hot oven.

ROLLS MADE OF RYE

Take a part of any of the given rye bread doughs, divide in one and a half ounce pieces, mould them in oblong pointed ovals, set on flour dusted boards; let raise about one-third. Transfer to peel which must be dusted with corn meal or flour and bake in a hot oven on the hearth. Wash over with water before baking and with a thin cornstarch wash, when they are taken out of the oven.

BUNS

Make a straight stiff dough of three quarts of water, half milk, at a temperature of eighty-five degrees Fahrenheit, four ounces of salt and twelve ounces of butter. Cover and let set in a warm place to double its size. When ready fold over and press down. Let come up again and fold over another time. Scale off a part of this dough to one pound pieces; divide these in eight equal parts; mould them round and arrange on greased baking sheets, leaving enough distance between them so as not to touch each other when baking. Let rise well and bake in a medium hot oven. After baking wash over with a thin syrup.

FANCY BUNS

SNAILS AND TWISTS

From the remaining dough, roll out a square flat piece one-eighth of an inch in thickness, brush the surface over with melted butter. Bestrew this with a mixture of granulated sugar and ground cinnamon, also Sultana raisins and currants. Fold the square from one side in the exact center; fold the other half on top of the other so as to form three succeeding layers. The dough will have now a long square shape. Turn it on the table's edge and roll a little thinner. Cut into strips about eight inches in length and half an inch wide. Roll these strips in the form of a jelly roll so that the three layers appear on the top of the roll, press the end piece under it and fasten well. Set on greased baking sheets so as not to touch each other; let set well and bake in a medium hot oven. Brush over with syrup when baked. When these buns have been properly rolled and placed on the pans they will raise higher in the middle than on the sides. Use only half of the strips for snails.

TWISTS

From the other half of the strips make twists in taking hold of both ends and fold as to form two equal parts side by side. Twist them over one another about four inches in length. Set on pans like the others and bake and finish in prescribed manner.

HOT CROSS BUNS

The same dough as for the other buns can be used. In four pound pieces of dough, work one pound of currants and Sultana raisins, mixed if desired; about four ounces of finely cut orange peel may also be worked into it. Some people prefer only to use currants. Let set as soon as the raisins are well worked in then divide in two ounce pieces, mould round, arrange on pans and cut when half set, a cross on top with a sharp knife or make this with a sharp tin formed in cross shape, pressing it through the center of the bun.

SALLY LUN

Scale off the same bun dough eight ounce pieces; mould them round and place in greased rings, which were previously put on baking sheets. The rings should be four and a half inches in diameter and four inches high. As soon as the rings are all filled make a hole in the center of each with the aid of a stick or with the finger. Let set to almost the height of the ring and bake in medium oven. When done wash over with syrup.

RAISIN LOAF

Weigh off the same bun dough, pieces of one pound, work in each of them a half pound of Sultana raisins. Mould round or in oblong oval shape, let set to double its volume; bake and finish exactly like preceding ones.

DRESDEN STOLLEN OR CHRISTMAS STOLLEN

Of ten pounds of a good strong wheat flour, half a pound of yeast, one pound and four ounces of sugar, two ounces of salt, five eggs and ten egg yolks, the grated rind of two lemons, one ounce of ground mace, three pounds of butter, five pounds raisins, one pound blanched almonds and one pound finely cut half citron and half orange peel, make a very stiff dough as follows: Dissolve the yeast in some lukewarm milk about three quarts to one gallon, the amount of milk to be used depends entirely on the strength of the flour; add the sugar, salt, eggs whole and yolks, lemon rind and mace and draw in the flour. Should the paste be not stiff enough you may add some more flour, but it is advisable to use rather a little less milk, so if necessary more milk can be added; work this dough over several times in small pieces, not more than one pound, putting one on top of each other and smoothing it down. When ready put to rise for about two

hours, mix in the butter first, working it well into the dough, then the almonds, peel, and add raisins. Let stand for one hour, throw out of the bowl and divide in the desired weight as two, three or four pounds; form long ovals of them, press down in center lengthwise with a very thin rolling pin, rolling it out flat about one inch and a half in the pressed down center; brush the thick outer sides over with butter and fold like a pocket book. Set to rise for half an hour in a warm place; wash over with a thin egg wash and bake in a medium warm oven. When baked, ice with a thick water icing. They can be kept for a length of time as they improve with age. In Europe, this Stollen is made some time before Christmas and served only on this day, hence the name Christmas Stollen.

STANDARD DOUGH FOR DIFFERENT COFFEE CAKES

Make rather a stiff dough from one pound of flour, two ounces of yeast, a pinch of salt, one ounce and a half of sugar, a pinch of ground mace, grated lemon rind, two eggs and lukewarm milk. Set to prove; when double its volume, work two ounces of butter into it, beating the dough well to admit plenty of air. When it ceases to adhere to the hand, it is ready for use. According to the amount of goods to be made, this dough can be increased to the quantity needed.

SMALL CAKES FOR COFFEE OR TEA PARTIES

Take one pound of the ready dough and work another two ounces of butter well into it. Let rise and scale off in half pound pieces; divide these pieces again in twelve equal parts; mould them round and let rise a while. Shape different formed small rolls of these pieces, bestrew them with either finely hacked blanched almonds, coarse granulated sugar or both almonds and sugar together, or cocoanut. The forms may be oval, round, very long and thin like finger rolls, ovals with pointed ends, "S" shape and others. When they are moulded, set on greased pans and let rise; wash them over with an egg wash and bestrew with the sugar or almonds, etc. Some may be only washed and when baked, can be iced with water icing while they are hot. Must rise double its size and be baked in a warm oven.

SNAILS

One pound of the standard dough; roll out to a very thin square about one-eighth of an inch in thickness; then roll out three ounces of puff paste, half the size of the square and place this on top of the puff paste. Flatten out two ounces of cold butter as thin as possible. Now fold the other half of the dough sheet over the other to cover all and to form a double sheet. This sheet is rolled out like puff paste, three times, give about ten minutes rest between each rolling, keeping the paste in a cold place. When finished, roll this dough out in a long square piece, length to be double the width. Brush this square over with melted butter; bestrew with sugar, mixed with cinnamon and some currants. Roll up like a jelly roll and fasten the outer edge securely and wash over with egg wash. See that the roll is of equal thickness all over. Cut into four equal parts andplace on greased baking sheet so as not to touch each other and press down a little with the flat of the hand. The upper side must show the rolling of the snail. Let rise well and bake in medium oven. Ice while hot.

NUT BUND CAKE

Roll out one pound of standard dough to a small square, put four ounces of butter, flatten out thin, on one side of the square, fold the other side over the butter and give three rollings like puff paste in ten minute intervals. Let rest for a while after the last rolling. Roll out in a square, must be the size of the mould when fastened in a circle as the mould used must be a Guggelhupf form. Wash the square over with a little egg wash on the outer edge and spread a mixture of two ounces roasted nuts ground fine, three ounces of cake crumbs, sifted through a small sieve and some milk to make a soft paste over it. Roll up like jelly roll, fasten the one end of the roll well in the other and place in a we l buttered and with finely shaved almond bestrewn mold. Set in a warm place to rise, let come up to two-thirds height of mould and bake in a medium warm oven. When baked, turn out of mould on a cake grate and before serving, dust well over with the finest powdered sugar.

PLAIN BUND GUGGELHUPF

Make a soft sponge with six ounces of flour and two ounces of yeast and set in a warm place to rise. During the time the sponge raises, heat in a bowl, using an egg whisk, five ounces of butter warmed up a little and one and a half ounces of sugar and seven egg yolks to a creamy mass; add a little salt, grated lemon rind, six ounces Sultana raisins, currants and finely cut orange peel. Mix and incorporate well with a wooden paddle. Mix six ounces of flour and the ready raised sponge into this preparation and at last, the seven whites of the eggs beaten to a stiff froth. Fill in a well buttered mould with tube in middle. Let rise and bake in medium oven. When baked and cold, ice with vanilla icing and strew some finely shaved browned almonds over the icing.

VANILLA COFFEE CAKE

Work in one pound of standard dough, one whole egg and two ounces of butter; when raised for about twenty minutes, roll out in thin sheet about a quarter of an inch thick; place on a greased baking sheet, taking care that the thickness is uniform all over. Prick with a fork in different places to prevent puffing up as the superfluous air on the bottom will escape. Let prove about two-thirds, wash over with egg wash and cover with granulated sugar mixed with a little vanilla sugar. Also cut from four ounces of sweet butter very small dices and place on top of the sugar in regular distances apart. Bake in a quick oven.

STREUSSELKUCHEN

Use the same dough as for vanilla coffee cake and roll out the same way, but before putting this cake to rise, wash over with egg wash and cover with the following mixture of Streussel: One pound of cake flour, half a pound of sugar, coffee sugar may be used, three of ground cinnamon. Rub all these ingredients well together and press through a coarse sieve, to form small balls. Should the mixture not hold well together and press through a coarse sieve, to form small balls a little more melted butter or milk may be added.

Another Streussel is made and is richer, consisting of four ounces of butter, three ounces of dry powdered almonds, four ounces of powdered sugar, half an ounce of ground cinnamon, lemon rind and twelve ounces of flour. Work the same way as preceding recipes. When the cake has raised, having been placed in a warm place, bake in a quick oven. When cold, dust over with fine powdered sugar.

GERMAN ROLLCOUCK

To one pound of standard dough, add six ounces of butter, work well in the dough, rather beating it in; set to rise. After having been set to rise, roll out and fill the same way as for snails; cut in thirty-two equal parts and set in well greased pound cake pans. These pans must have the same diameter on bottom as on top, straight a round. Place so in the pans as to form circles in the pan with the side showing the rollings upward. Let rise and bake in medium hot oven. When baked take from mould and ice with water icing while hot. As the rolls are set along side of each other, the cake when serving is not cut, but broken off, as the snails will be detached easily from each other.

DOUGH FOR FRUIT TARTS

Make a medium stiff dough from one pound of flour, two whole and three yolks of eggs; two ounces of yeast, a pinch of salt and one and a half ounces of sugar. Let rise to double its size, then work three ounces of butter well into the dough and let come up again.

Roll this dough in round flats, put on greased baking pans, (in Europe special made round single pans provided with only strong wire rim are in use), wash the edge with egg wash and paste well around evenly rolled quarter inch thick strip of dough. Put finely sifted cake crumbs on top of these bottoms and also a little sugar. Fill these rounds with any desired cleaned fresh fruit; put more sugar on top, adding the flavors as cinnamon, mace, etc., which are best suited for the selected fruit. Brush over the rim well with egg wash and place larger flats, which must be first folded in four and marked in the center with a few cuts on top, cutting them nicely round and pressing them on the washed border. The protruding dough must be pushed and fastened under the bottoms. Let rise and bake in a medium oven, must be brushed over with egg wash before baking. To cut the bottoms nice and round use a cake ring; place on top of the flat piece and cut around outside the ring with a very sharp knife.

GREEK BREAD (Pam'a'la'Grecque)

Make a rather slack dough of four pounds of flour, three ounces of yeast, two ounces of sugar, half an ounce of salt, half an ounce of ground cinnamon and lukewarm milk. Cover and let rise to double its size. When ready add one pound of butter and one pound of lard. Beat both well in the paste and let come up again. Scale off in three ounce pieces; roll out, putting them in granulated sugar in round strips, the length of the width of a baking sheet. Place on greased pans about one-quarter inch apart and let rise to double its size; bake in cool oven to a nice crisp. When baked cut in three inch pieces; cut them while warm.

ROLLCOUCKS AND CRAMICK

Make a rather stiff dough from one pound and a half of flour, six eggs and sufficient warm milk, work it well and smooth. Add then three ounces of yeast dissolved in a little milk or water, incorporate well in the dough, cover and let rise in a warm place. When well risen, work into it six ounces of butter in which a pinch of salt and two ounces of sugar were mixed. Beat the dough well; cover again and let come up another time. Scale off a few half pound pieces and form into oblong ovals. You may add a few Sultana raisins in each piece before moulding into shape. Place on greased baking sheets, let rise double its size and before baking, wash over with egg wash and cut with sharp pair of scissors, dipped in hot water, all around about half an inch above the bottom. Care must be taken so as to cut an even and straight incision. In baking this cake will show a nice whitish border all around. Ice with water icing while hot. These cakes are called Cramick.

ROLLCOUCK

Of the remaining dough roll out a long strip an eighth of an inch thick and nine inches wide. Brush over with water or egg wash and cover with a mixture of sugar and cinnamon, also strew over with some currants; fold one side over the middle and the other on top of the first fold; roll lightly over with rolling pin. To obtain three inch pieces in length, cut in squares two inches wide. Set on pans, let rise, wash with egg wash and bake in a warm oven. Ice with water icing when done and while warm.

BERLIN PANCAKE

Make a medium stiff dough of one pound of flour, two ounces of yeast, a pinch of salt, grated lemon rind, one and a half ounces of sugar and lukewarm milk. Let rise to double its volume; add then three ounces of butter, beating the dough well, set to prove. When ready scale off in half pound pieces; divide these in eight equal parts and set on well flour dusted boards after having them moulded round. Cover and let rise. When raised, press a hole in the middle with your finger and place a little raspberry jam in the hollows. Pinch them well together without washing so they form again a round ball, set them back on the boards and let rise to double their size. In the meantime have an iron pot or casserole filled with half lard and half butter and set on fire to heat. When hot enough, the pancakes are baked in it turning them from time to time. The color will be rather brown. It is essential that the grease is not too hot as the cakes will not bake in the center and will also be black instead of brown. As soon as they come from the pan roll in granulated sugar. Use a skimmer in taking the cakes from the grease and let the grease run off well.

When the pancakes are filled and pinched they must be so perfectly closed so as not to let the marmalade run out while baking. The sugar contained in the jam will add much to the coloring while cooking; also set the finished cakes back on the boards with the pinched side down.

BRIOCHE

Make a sponge medium stiff of four ounces of flour and two ounces of yeast; mould this sponge round and make a cross incision on top. Put this sponge in a small vessel filled half full of lukewarm water. During the time the sponge rises, make a medium stiff paste of eight ounces of flour, four to five eggs, a little milk, a pinch of salt, one ounce of sugar. Work this dough well with both hands, beating it on the table to incorporate plenty of air and obtain a very smooth paste; add nine ounces of sweet butter, repeating the same beating as before for five minutes. Then mix the sponge well with the dough and set to rise over night in an ice box or on ice. In the morning divide in one and a half ounce pieces; mould them round and let rest for a while before putting them in the greased tartlet moulds. Make a top to the round pieces in holding the hand so as to roll on the table a very small ball held by a tiny piece of dough to the bigger body of the Brioche. Let rise well, wash over with egg wash and cut four incisions from the sides of the Brioche to the middle, not touching the small head. This must be done with the scissors dipped in warm water. Bake in good warm oven. Mostly used for breakfast, also for afternoon teas—toasted and buttered.

The Brioches can be also baked on pans; proceed as follows: Divide in one and quarter ounce pieces and leave enough paste to be able to make the heads of the Brioche. Mould the pieces round, divide the rest of the dough for the heads in as many equal very small pieces as you have Brioches. Set the large moulded rounds right off on greased pans. The small ones let rise on another cloth covered board. When ready, wash over the Brioche with egg wash; put the small balls on top in the center of each, cut four incisions with scissors, not touching the head of the Brioche. Incisions should mark across and are cut with the scissors, holding one point of the scissors under the bottom of the large round piece and cutting it through from the top.

MASARIN

Masarin is made of Savarin dough and baked in pound cake mould with sloping side. The mould is greased as stated for Savarin and finely shaved almonds put on the bottom. Fill half full and let come up to the top of the mould; bake in a medium hot oven. When baked and cold, soak in a thin syrup with only vanilla flavor in it. Before soaking, cut off the top of the cake, it being the part with the almonds showing. Cut about a quarter of an inch from the top. In the bottom part, make a hole about half an inch deep, leave a border about a quarter of an inch thick, so it will be strong enough to hold the cream filling. When cut, soak the whole cake using a brush and cover the top part with hot apricot sauce, also using a brush.

Cream Filling

Soak your leaves of gelatine in cold water. During the time the gelatine softens, cook one quart of milk and pour the boiling milk slowly in a well beaten preparation of four ounces of sugar, one ounce of strong flour and four egg yolks. Return to the casserole and bring all to a boil. As soon as cooked, add the gelatine, mixing it well, let stand to cool. In the meantime, beat four egg whites and mix well under the almost cold cream. Fill in the Masarin and when stiffened, place the cover on top. The cream must be about half an inch above the border and must show when cover is put on.

PLAIN BUNS

To five pounds of sponge, add one gill of milk, half a pound of sugar, half an ounce of salt, a little mace and grated rind of one lemon. Mix these ingredients well into the sponge, add enough flour to make a smooth dough and then add half a pound of lard and work all well together. Let rise to only half its volume and make up in round buns, one and a half ounces in weight; set on greased pans and bake in medium hot oven, wash before baking with egg wash.

OPERA BUNS

Divide the bun dough in one and a half ounce pieces, mould first round and after a little rest, roll in form of finger rolls; place on greased pans, so as to touch each other on the sides but not on the ends. Let rise. When ready brush over with a light egg wash and sprinkle finely chopped nuts on top. Bake and when taken from the oven, ice with vanilla flavored stiff water icing.

COCOANUT BUNS

Mould one pound of fresh grated cocoanut and vanilla flavor in five pounds of bun dough, let rise. Divide in one and a half ounce pieces; mould first round and after a while in small, pointed oval loaves. Set on pans, so as not to touch each other on the sides. Let rise and bake in a good heat. When baked, ice with water icing and besprinkle with slightly browned grated cocoanut.

COFFEE CAKES WITH SPONGE

Make a stiff sponge with two quarts of warm milk and four ounces of yeast. When fallen in center mix thoroughly, one quart of warm milk, six eggs, one pound and four ounces of sugar, half an ounce salt, mace and lemon flavor and enough flour to obtain a rather stiff dough. At last work one pound and a half of flour well into it and make coffee cakes of it.

STREUSSELKUCHEN-GERMAN STYLE

To one part of the coffee cake dough, add some currants, Sultana raisins and chopped almonds. Scale off in half pound pieces, mould round and let stand for a while. Flatten this round with the hand and roll out with the rolling pin in round flats, one-quarter inch thick. Brush over with egg wash and cover with Streussel; let rise double the size and bake in good hot oven.

GERMAN STREUSSEL

Rub together one pound powdered sugar, one pound and four ounces cake flour, eight ounces of butter, two ounces chopped almonds, lemon flavor and powdered cinnamon. When well rubbed it should form in small round balls. The better way is to press it through a coarse sieve.

CINNAMON CAKE

Prepare the same way as the Streussel cake, brush over with melted butter and cover with a thick layer of sugar mixed with powdered cinnamon. Bake like the Streusselkuchen.

ALMOND COFFEE CAKE

To four pounds of coffee cake dough, add one pound of chopped almonds, roll out pieces of two pounds in squares half an inch thick. Place on baking sheets; wash with egg wash and bake. When baked, ice over with water icing and sprinkle with chopped and browned almonds.

GERMAN APPLE CAKE

Roll out a thin sheet of the coffee cake dough one-eighth inch in thickness, to cover a baking sheet; press all the sides well up to form a border and give a little time to rise. Peel some good baking apples, cut each apple in eight pieces and take out the kernels; place nicely in rows on top of this sheet, besprinkle with sugar and cinnamon also a few currants and finely chopped citron peel; cover with a well greased sheet of strong paper and bake in a medium oven. All kinds of fruit cake can be made with the same dough and in the same manner. For peaches, apricots and plums, stone the fruit and cut in halves; arrange nicely and sprinkle sugar over. Berries as well as cherries are used. Whole cherries must also be stoned; berries should be washed and picked over. For berry cakes, as blueberries, make a thin custard cream, pour it over and bake with the cake.

CHEESE CAKE

Roll out a flat round ten ounces of coffee cake dough and line a well greased cake ring with it. Set the ring on a baking sheet, prick a little with a fork and fill with the following mixture: Rub one pound and four ounces of firm cheese with three ounces of sugar, three ounces of flour, and add five egg yolks, rubbing all the time, a pinch of salt, vanilla flavor is also added. When smooth soften with a little milk and mix two ounces butter, some cleaned currants and five whites of eggs beaten to a stiff froth into the former preparation. Bake about half an hour in a good heat. As soon as the cake has risen, cut all around the border with a very sharp knife.

GUGGELHUPF

Make a soft sponge of four ounces of flour and half an ounce of yeast and a little warm milk. Let rise in a warm place. In the meantime while the sponge is setting beat three ounces of sugar with half a pound of butter to a creamy froth; add fourteen egg yolks, four at a time, beating constantly. When the sponge is ready add to this mixture, twelve ounces of flour and the sponge, work every thing well together and put in a well buttered Guggelhupf mould; let rise and bake. When baked and cold, sift some very fine powdered sugar over.

ZWIEBACK

From a piece of bun dough mould round pieces about one ounce in weight; after a rest of about ten minutes, form in finger rolls three inches long. Arrange these fingers side by side close together in rows on a greased baking sheet; let rise double its size, wash over with a thin egg wash and bake.

Let the baked Zwieback stand until the next day, then cut in slices, arrange on pans and toast them in the oven to a nice golden color. Some of the Zwieback may be iced with the following white of egg icing: Mix white of eggs with finest powdered sugar to a medium stiff paste; add a few drops of lemon juice and beat very light; spread this icing very thin and even over the Zwieback, using a knife. Put in oven, to give a nice light brown color. Finely shaved almonds can also be sprinkled over the icing and baked with it.

PRETZELS

Roll twenty ounces of coffee cake dough into a sheet, spread six ounces of butter of the same consistency as the dough on one side and cover the other half over the first; the butter being inside. Roll out like puff paste and fold in three, by bringing one side in the center of the dough and covering with the other side. Take particular care that all three layers are equal size and cover each other perfectly even. Let rest for fifteen minutes in a cold place and give two more rollings in the same intervals. When rested after the last folding roll out in a sheet half an inch thick and cut in narrow strips. Twist each strip taking hold of the opposite ends and roll,with one hand towards you and the other from it; place on greased pans, set to prove and bake in a good heat. Ice with vanilla water icing as soon as they are taken from the oven and besprinkle with shaved browned almonds.

CHEESE CAKE BAKED IN SQUARES

Line a baking sheet with coffee cake dough an eighth of an inch thick, edges must be raised to form a border and keep the cheese preparation from running out:

Cheese mixture— rub six ounces of butter, eight ounces of sugar, and three pounds of dry cheese curd to a very smooth paste; add three ounces of flour, and eight eggs, rub again well together and at last a pinch of salt, mace, grated lemon rind, half a pint of milk, six ounces currants and six ounces of Sultana raisins. When mixed thoroughly, spread evenly over the dough and bake in a medium hot oven. When cold sift sugar and cinnamon on top. Raisins and currants may be omitted in the mixture, but a few currants may be sprinkled over the cheese before baking.

SALT STICKS

Make a firm dough of one pound of flour, a pinch of salt, one ounce and a half of yeast and lukewarm milk; use good strong flour. When the dough has set, work six ounces of butter well into it and let rise again. Divide in small pieces, roll out to a very thin quarter of an inch thick long round strips. Place them on a greased baking sheet and place the strips a little distance apart across the width of the pan and give half proof. Before baking brush over with water and besprinkle thickly with salt. When baked, cut in sticks, three inches in length. Cut while warm.

YEAST RAISED DOUGHNUTS

Roll out a piece of ready bun dough to a sheet half an inch thick, cut with a doughnut cutter. Place in cloth lined, flour dusted boxes and let rise. Heat in a flat cruller frying pan some lard, or lard and butter mixed and fry to a nice brown color. Do not give too much proof and have the grease hot, but not too hot. Cold grease will soak too much in the doughnuts and will absolutely spoil them. Take them out of the grease with a skimmer, let the superfluous grease drip off and roll in granulated sugar, mixed with a little cinnamon.

BAKING POWDER DOUGHNUTS

Four pounds of flour, one and a half pounds of sugar, six ounces of butter, one ounce cream tartar, half an ounce of baking soda, eight eggs, one and a half pints of milk a little mace and lemon extract. Sift cream of tartar with the flour on a sheet of paper, cream sugar and butter together, rub in the eggs, add a flavoring and the milk in which soda must be dissolved just before the milk is put into the mixture, work all well together and mix in the flour.

Roll out to a sheet and cut with doughnut cutter, fry like other doughnuts and dust over with sugar. Instead of cream of tartar and soda, two ounces of baking powder may be used, which must be sifted with the flour. When using sour instead of sweet milk, add one ounce and a half of baking soda into the milk, leaving out cream of tartar and baking powder.

FRENCH CRULLERS

Put one pint of water and half a pound of butter together on the fire in a deep saucepan. Sift one pound of flour and two ounces of sugar on a sheet of paper. When water is boiling and rises, mix the flour in, stirring quickly. Leave, while stirring, on fire until the preparation does not stick to the casserole; work into this paste while warm, fifteen eggs, two by two at a time. Put the paste in a lady finger bar provided with a large star tube; dress on round cut and greased papers, the size of diameter of frying pan, in rings. When the grease is hot, turn the cakes with the paper on them, the paper side up; it can be removed after a short while. The rings must be turned several times during the frying process to bake evenly to

a nice brown color. They may be served hot or cold with whipped cream or another cream sauce.

ENGLISH CRUMPETS

Make a slack dough of one quart of lukewarm milk, half an ounce of salt, one ounce of yeast and about two and a half pounds of good flour. Let set and work well again. Set to rise again, when ready, mold round and arrange in cloth lined, well floured boxes; let rise and bake in greased rings, flatten them in stretching lightly, but keep in shape. When baked to a nice brown color on one side, lift the crumpet and ring carefully and turn over on the other side, finish baking. The dough can also be made with half water and half milk instead of all milk.

MUFFINS

Muffins may be made of medium firm milk bread dough. Flatten a piece of dough with the hands about half an inch in thickness and cut with a cake cutter three inches in diameter; set on lightly floured boards or baking sheets and let prove half its height. Bake without rings on griddle to a nice brown color on both sides; put on baking sheets and bake for five minutes in the oven.

Muffins when cold can be cut in halves, toasted and buttered. When served hot they should be broken open and buttered; crumpets are prepared the same way. Milk or cream may also be served with both.

CRUMPETS (Very soft Mixture)

Make a soft batter of two pounds of flour, one quart milk, half an ounce of salt and one of yeast. It should be thickly running batter; let set like a bread sponge until it drops in center, beat it well down again and let come up only half. Grease griddle as well as rings, set the rings on the griddle plate and fill the batter in them with a custard dipper provided with a spout. Bake on side and turn carefully with the ring over on the other side, using a cake turner.

WHEAT MUFFINS

Sift on a sheet of paper one ounce and a half of baking powder together with two ounces of cake flour. Rub eight ounces of butter and five ounces of sugar to a frothy cream, add gradually five eggs, beating all the time, mix a pinch of salt, mace and one quart of milk well into it and add the flour. Divide in greased muffin rings, placed on a greased baking sheet. Let rise and bake in a medium hot oven. They may also be baked in greased muffin cups.

CORN MUFFINS

Sift two ounces of baking powder with one and a half pounds of flour. Add one pound of yellow corn meal to it and mix well together. Cream eight ounces of butter and twelve ounces of sugar, rub into this, eight eggs, two at a time, mix one quart of milk and make a slack dough with the flour. Divide in muffin pans and bake in a good heat. Should make three dozen muffins.

POPOVERS

Beat four eggs, a pinch of salt and one pint of milk together and pour this in half a pound of flour gradually, stirring well to get a smooth running paste free from lumps; pass through a strainer and fill in well greased high timball moulds, the moulds should be a little more than half full. Bake for about thirty minutes in a medium hot oven.

TEA BISCUITS

Rub three ounces of lard and three ounces of butter, also three ounces of baking powder, well with six pounds of cake flour; add three pints of milk, a little salt and mix to a soft dough; do not work the dough too much, to prevent it from being too tough. Roll out about half an inch thick and set on greased baking pan close together. Let stand for about fifteen minutes. Brush over with egg wash and bake in a good heat; when baked and while hot, brush over with melted lard or butter.

SANDWICH ROLLS

The same preceding dough is divided in one and a half ounce pieces, moulded round like rolls and formed to oblong ovals with pointed ends. Let rest for at least twenty minutes, brush with egg wash and bake.

SCONS

The tea biscuit dough is scaled off in one pound pieces and moulded round after a few minutes rest, roll out with a thin rolling pin, the size of a pie plate; place on greased baking sheets and cut crosswise with the dough scraper. Let stand fifteen minutes, prick a little with a fork, brush over with egg wash and bake in a good heat. Scons are generally broken open and buttered. Serve hot.

IMITATION FRENCH ROLLS WITH BAKING POWDER

Make a tea biscuit dough of two pounds of flour, two and a half ounces baking powder, one ounce and a half of sugar, half an ounce of melted lard or butter, two egg yolks and one pint of milk, good measure. Rub all ingredients dry with the flour and add the milk last. Let this dough rest a few minutes, cut in one and a half ounce pieces, mould round, let rest again and press lengthwise through the middle, greasing the tops a little before making the split. Arrange on baking sheets, brush over with melted lard, let stand for twenty minutes to rise and bake in a good warm oven.

CORN BREAD

Scald twelve ounces of white corn meal with one pint of boiling water, add three ounces of melted lard or butter, half an ounce of salt, half a pint of cold milk and two eggs. Mix in four ounces of white corn meal and one ounce of baking powder; stir all well together with an egg whisk. The pan in which it is baked, must be heated well, while preparing the dough; it should be like a thin batter and about an inch and a half deep in the pan. Bake half an hour or more. When the pan is very hot no greasing is needed.

GRIDDLE CAKES AND WAFFLES

Griddle cakes and waffles may be made with yeast as well as baking powder. Baking powder cakes do not require as much time as yeast raised cakes, but griddle cakes made with yeast are the better ones. The griddle plate and the waffle irons must be clean, well greased and hot, to avoid sticking and burning.

WHEAT CAKES

Sift one pound of wheat flour, three ounces of sugar, a little salt and one ounce of baking powder together; mix with enough milk to make a thin running batter, add three well beaten eggs and one ounce melted butter. When a larger quantity is called for, leave the baking powder out of the preparation and only add it to the batter when baking begins; it is advisable to mix in half of the batter the necessary amount of powder and when exhausted, prepare the second half for use. When baking the plate should be hot, but not too hot, so the cakes can bake thoroughly in center. Serve with syrup as soon as done.

WHEAT CAKES WITH YEAST

Make a very soft sponge as for crumpets with two pounds of flour, three ounces of yeast and two quarts of warm water; let stand until it falls in center, beat well, add one tablespoonful of syrup, four well beaten eggs, a pinch of salt and four ounces of melted butter, beat all well together; let rise a little and bake.

GRAHAM BATTER CAKES WITH POWDER

Sift in two pounds of wheat flour, three ounces of baking powder; mix two pounds of unsifted graham flour well with it, add half a pint of molasses, four well beaten eggs, one teaspoonful of salt, four ounces of melted butter and enough milk to make a smooth batter.

GRAHAM CAKES WITH YEAST

Make a soft sponge of one pound of graham flour and one pound wheat flour mixed; three ounces of yeast, and one quart of warm water; beat back when it drops in center, then add two ounces of syrup, salt, two well beaten eggs and two ounces melted butter. Let rise a little and bake. When sponge is set over night it must be mixed with cold water.

BUCKWHEAT CAKES WITH YEAST

From one pound of buckwheat flour, four ounces of corn flour, two ounces of sugar, one teaspoonful of salt and one quart of warm water, make a smooth soft batter; dissolve three-quarters of an ounce of yeast in a little warm water and add to the batter; heat everything well together; let rise for about four hours, or until it drops in center, then add a tablespoonful of molasses and proceed as for the other cakes. When ready to use, add two teaspoonfuls of baking powder to half of the batter and when it is all used up, prepare the other half the same way. The same recipe may be used for baking powder cakes.

BUCKWHEAT CAKES

To four pounds of buckwheat flour add four ounces of baking powder and half a teaspoonful of baking soda; mix with milk, half water, to a smooth soft batter; then incorporate one ounce of salt, half a pint of molasses and four ounces of butter.

FLANNEL CAKES

Rub four ounces of butter and two ounces of sugar to a cream, add four eggs, one by one, rubbing all the time. Mix into this half a pound of wheat flour and two gills of milk to make a smooth batter; before using beat one tablespoonful of baking powder well in the batter.

INDIAN GRIDDLE CAKES

Make a smooth batter of six ounces wheat flour, four ounces of corn meal, one ounce of powdered sugar, a pinch of salt and one gill of milk. Mix into this one and a half ounces of melted butter and just before baking, one teaspoonful of baking powder mixed with a little flour.

RICE CAKES

Sift together four ounces of wheat flour and four ounces of rice flour, put in a bowl and make a hollow in center, place in this two ounces of sugar, a pinch of salt, four beaten eggs and one gill of milk. Make a smooth dough from these ingredients and when well mixed add one more gill of milk, finally pour into this two ounces of melted butter and half a pint well cooked dry rice. Beat in a teaspoonful of baking powder just before using.

WAFFLES

Beat one-quarter of a pound of powdered sugar well with sixteen whole eggs, add one quart of milk and mix two pounds and four ounces of flour into this, to obtain a smooth paste, free from lumps, beat then twelve ounces of melted butter, a pinch of salt, mace or lemon flavor well into the batter and mix two heaping teaspoonfuls of baking powder to the whole preparation. Bake in hot well greased waffle irons.

CREAM WAFFLES

Beat twelve ounces of butter well with ten whole and six yolks of eggs, add three ounces of sugar, lemon flavor and one and a half pounds of wheat flour. Into this mix slowly, one pint of whipped cream and six whites of eggs, beaten to a stiff froth.

WAFFLES A'LA BOURGEOISE

Cream half a pound of butter with eight eggs well, add a pinch of salt and one pound of flour; mix with enough milk into a thin batter as for pancakes. Bake in very hot irons and dust after baking well with sugar.

HOLLAND WAFFLES

Make a sponge of twelve ounces of flour, one and a half ounces of sugar, a pinch of salt, grated lemon rind, three eggs, six ounces melted butter, two ounces of yeast and one pint of lukewarm sweet cream; let set, beat and let rise a little again and bake as usual. Sift over with sugar and cinnamon mixed.

FRENCH SWEET WAFFLES

Separate fourteen eggs, sift together six ounces of sugar, one pound of flour and a little salt, put in a bowl and make a hollow in center. Beat the fourteen yolks of eggs with milk well together and make a smooth batter with the flour, add half a cup of brandy and one ounce of melted butter. When proceeding to make, mix into this batter one pint of whipped cream and the stiffly beaten fourteen whites of eggs. If batter must stand long, add a little baking powder.

RICE WAFFLES

Make a smooth batter of one quart of soft boiled rice, one and a half pints of milk, one pound of flour, six eggs, one teaspoonful of salt, one spoonful of melted butter, one spoonful of syrup and two teaspoonfuls of baking powder.

NEWPORT WAFFLES

Make a mush of one pint of Indian meal in the usual way; while hot, add a small lump of butter and a teaspoonful of salt; let cool. Beat separately in the meantime, four eggs, add them to the mush and stir gradually into the preparation, one quart of flour. Add also, a half pint of buttermilk or sour cream in which a half a teaspoonful of soda is dissolved. Stir all well together and mix milk enough into it to obtain a thin batter and bake as usual.

Franz G. Bock

PASTRIES

JEAN S. BERDOU
CHEF DE CUISINE
HOTEL ASTOR
New York City, N. Y.

Mr. Berdou took his apprenticeship under the celebrated Argeles Gasost, chef at the Hotel de France, Paris, after which he was with the Hotel Continental at Cauterets, France, Hotel de France at Paris, Hotel Continental, Biarritz, France and Restaurant Francais, Madrid, Spain. Coming to this country he was at the famous Louis Sherry's Cafe, New York City.

BEIGNETS DE POMMES (Apple Fritters)

Make a paste with four-fifths pound of flour, four whole eggs, two pinches of salt, a spoonful sugar, one pint milk. Take four whites of eggs, well beaten, and mix with paste. Peel four apples, cut in round slices of medium thickness. Put in bowl with a little sugar and cognac and let soak for a few mi utes, then drop apples in paste above mentioned and fry in hot grease. Serve on napkin with vanilla flavored powdered sugar.

PANCAKE A LA CONFITURE

Take one and one-half ounces flour, four yolks of eggs, two whole eggs, one pint of uncooked milk, three tablespoonfuls of powdered sugar and a little salt. Mix the whole to medium paste, ad l one pony glass of cognac and a few chopped bitter almonds. Take clean frying pan, butter it lightly, and pour the paste on it, so it will divide equally all over the pan and fry to a golden brown. Take a spoonful of good jelly, spread on pan cakes and roll them up and serve. This recipe should make at least twenty-four pancakes.

Jean Berdou

JEAN JUILLARD

CHEF DE CUISINE

HOTEL ADOLPHUS

Dallas, Tex.

Mr. Juillard was formerly at Cafe Anglais, Paris; Hotel Hermitage, Monte Carlo; Hotel d'Angleterre, Venice; Savoy Hotel and Princess Restaurant, London; the Plaza, Belmont and Astor Hotels, New York City; Hotel La Salle, Rector's Cafe and University Club, Chicago.

WAFFLES MACONNAISE

On ordinary waffles, paste with a sabayon, as follows: Have prepared some fresh grapes, skinned and seeds removed; some brandied cherries, cut in dice; a port wine glass full of Hennessey brandy; the yolks of six eggs; one-half pint of good cream; sugar to suit taste. Mix the sugar and yolks of eggs together; add the grapes, cherries and cream, which have been boiled; then cook until near boiling; add your cognac; place all in a china bowl and mix until almost cold.

J. Juillard

HENRI BERGER

CHEF DE CUISINE

FRANKFURTER-HOF

Frankfurt,

A. M. Germany

Mr. Berger has been with the following hotels: Hotel Chatham, Paris; the Hermitage at Monte Carlo, France; the Grand Hotel des Thermes, Salsomaggiore, Italy; the famous Hotel Ritz, Paris, prior to coming to the Frankfurter-hof.

CHESTER CAKE

Proportions: three and one-half ounces of flour, same of butter, one and three-fourth ounce grated Parmesan, three yolks of eggs. Mix whole, but don't give it too much body. Spread thin on baking pan, let cool for one hour and cut in strips of one and one-half inches in diameter and bake in moderate oven

Henri Berger

CHAS. GROLIMUND
CHEF DE CUISINE
WASHINGTON HOTEL
Seattle, Wash.

Mr. Grolimund was formerly at the Grand Hotel Neues Stahlbad, St. Moritz-Bad; Grand Hotel Brussels, Brussels; Grand Hotel Quirinal, Rome; Grand Hotel Anatre Nation, Barcelona, Restaurant Delmonico, New York and the St. Francis, San Francisco.

BASLER LECKERLI (Eight covers)

Two pounds honey, two pounds sugar, four pounds flour, two pounds almonds, one-half pound citron, one-half pound orange peel, one-half quart water; one-fourth ounce cinnamon, cloves and nutmeg, two finely chopped lemon rinds, one-half pint kirschwasser; one-fourth ounce almonds finely powdered.

Heat the honey and water first, then mix with the other ingredients, forming a dough. Roll out on a greased baking sheet to about one-eighth inch thickness and bake in a medium hot oven until well browned. When done, ice with Italian meringue and cut into uniform oblongs.

Charles Grolimund

GEORGE E. SCHAAF
CHEF DE CUISINE
HOTEL ALBANY
Denver, Colo.

Mr. Schaaf has been connected with several prominent hotels in this country prior to coming to the Albany, and was at one time, Chef at the Minneapolis Club in Minneapolis.

ENGLISH MUFFINS

Two quarts of milk, one and one-half ounces yeast, one ounce salt. Work into a medium dough and let set one hour. Work out again and mould the size of an egg and flatten a little. Now let rest until twice its size and bake on cake griddle.

Geo. E. Schaaf

EMILE BAILLY,
CHEF DE CUISINE
HOTEL ST. REGIS
New York City, N.Y.

Mr. Bailly prior to coming to this country served in the very best hotels in Europe. He left the Grand Hotel of Monte Carlo, France ten years ago, to come to New York and open the St. Regis.

GAUFRETTE SUISSE

Five ounces flour, five ounces granulated sugar, two and one-half ounces drawn butter, one egg, two soupspoonfuls warm milk. Melt the sugar in the milk, then put flour, egg, butter, mix well together. Must be hard enough to be worked with the roller (it is better to make the dough the day before). Make twelve or fourteen little balls, about the size of a walnut. Flatten a little with roller, put on pastry pan and bake in the oven eight minutes.

PANCAKE HORTENSIA

Five ounces flour, three eggs, two ounces sugar, one teaspoonful salt, one ounce drawn butter, three cups milk. Take three eggs, one-half pound cream cheese, pass through the sifter, work well in a bowl with three yolks, juice of one-half orange, two soupspoonfuls of powdered sugar. Make twelve pancakes, five inches in diameter; place on each pancake one small spoonful of the said preparation. Add a few raisins. Roll the pancakes and lay them in a tureen. Pour over it the following cream: half quart cream, half orange juice, three spoonfuls powdered sugar, let boil slowly in an oven not too hot, for three-quarters of an hour. A few minutes before baking, put some sugar over it and brown.

Emile Bailly.

CESAR OBRECHT
CHEF DE CUISINE
GRAND HOTEL DE L'EUROPE
Lucerne, Switzerland
also
PALACE HOTEL LTD.
Murren, Switzerland

Mr. Obrecht, prior to holding his present position, was at the Grand Savoy Hotel at Florence, at the Grand Hotel and Kurhaus, at St. Blasien; the Grand Hotel de Thouwe at Thouwe, the Grand Hotel Krasnapolsky at Amsterdam, the Grand Hotel de Salines at Reinfelden and the Grand Hotel Waldhaus at Vulpera.

SOURAROFF

Four ounces flour, two ounces butter, one and one-half ounces fine sugar, one-halt pint cream, vanilla, form heap with flour and put rest of ingredients in center, mix together and let stand. Roll out paste and form flute, put in baking pan and bake in hot oven.

César Obrecht

MUFFINS

Half pound cornmeal, one-fourth pound flour, three-fourths pint milk, two eggs, tablespoon of yeast, one ounce good melted butter, one tablespoonful of honey, one teaspoonful salt, one tablespoonful of sugar, two ounces of currants. Make a smooth dough with both flour and milk, dissolve the yeast with a little milk and mix it in the dough. Put it in a bowl, cover with a towel and let rise in a warm place for one hour. Add the other ingredients. Work them all together for a good five minutes. Divide the paste into buttered muffin rings, let them rise again for another hour and cook in a moderate oven until thoroughly brown.

LOUIS LESCARBOURA
CHEF DE CUISINE
FT. PITT HOTEL
Pittsburg, Pa.

Prior to coming to the Fort Pitt Hotel, Mr. Lescarboura was Chef at the Hotel Marlborough, New York City, and other prominent eastern hotels, and was Entremetier at the famous "Delmonico's Cafe," New York City.

MARTIN GINDER
CHEF DE CUISINE
HOTEL GREEN
Pasadena, Cal.

Mr. Ginder was apprenticed in France in the best hotels. He was at the New York Athletic Club, the Princeton Club, the old Hotel Metropole, Cafe Savarin and the Vendome Hotel, New York City. He has also held several important positions in the middle west prior to taking his present position.

OLD FASHIONED GRIDDLE CAKES

One tablespoonful of butter, two eggs, two cupfuls of milk, one teaspoonful of salt and two teaspoonfuls of baking powder. Warm the butter in the milk, pour in the yolk of a well beaten egg, add sufficient flour to make it pour easily, then add the salt and baking powder. Whip the white of an egg and mix all together thoroughly. Bake on a hot griddle. Make the cakes a good size, spread granulated maple sugar between each cake and serve the cakes on a plate with a cake cover.

GOLD CAKE

Half cupful of butter, half cupful of sugar, five yolks of eggs, one teaspoonful orange extract, seven-eighths cupful of flour, one teaspoonful of baking powder, quarter cupful of milk. Cream the butter, add sugar slowly and continue beating. Add the yolks of five eggs beaten until thick. Add orange extract, mix and sift flour with the baking powder and add alternately with milk to the first mixture. Bake in buttered and floured tin.

APPLE PIE

Roll pie crust to the thickness desired. Place this on a pie dish, shaping it carefully and cut around the edges with a sharp knife. Cover the bottom of crust with a layer of sugar, dust with flour, then fill the crust with quarters of peeled and cored apples. Dust with a little salt and plenty of sugar. Cover the whole with the crust and trim the edges again. Press together upper and lower crust. Bake until apples are done, and bottom crust is a nice brown. Serve with every portion, a piece of American cheese.

SWEET CORN PUDDING

Scrape the corn from six ears, beat three eggs, and add one cupful of milk, half teaspoonful of salt, one dash of cayenne pepper, mix eggs in slightly with two tablespoonfuls of melted butter and a tablespoonful of sugar. Bake in deep small vegetable dish or custard cups for fifteen minutes, in a slow oven.

S. B. PETTENGILL
CHEF DE CUISINE
HOTEL ORMOND
Ormond Beach, Fla.

Mr. Pettengill has been chef at the Hotel Ormond for fifteen seasons, and at the Crawford House, White Mountains, N. H. for twenty-five seasons.

BEATEN BISCUIT

Take a quart of pastry flour and add one-half teaspoonful salt, sift and work two tablespoonfuls lard into the flour with the finger tips. Add enough cold water so as to make a stiff dough. Place dough on a bread board and beat for about twenty minutes with a mallet, then roll out, cut and place in a pan which has been greased, prick with a fork and bake in hot oven for twenty minutes. Serve piping hot.

HOT SPOON BREAD

Take one quart white corn meal into which has been sifted a tablespoonful of salt. Pour about a pint of scalding water on the meal and mix thoroughly. Put this mixture on a well greased pan with a spoon and place in hot oven to bake for fifteen minutes. Serve hot.

S. B. Pettengill

G. R. MEYER
CHEF
RECTOR'S
Chicago, Ill.
With finest hotels in Europe, also the Auditorium, Congress and College Inn, Chicago.

CORN BREAD

Put four ounces of butter into a mixing bowl, with four ounces of sugar and a pinch of salt, cream it well, then add four eggs, one at a time, beat well and add half a pint of milk. Mix, then add one pound of corn meal and half a pound of flour, adding two teaspoonfuls of baking powder to the flour before sifting. This may be baked in individual well buttered corn moulds or in a shallow buttered pan, filling from half to two-thirds full and baking from fifteen to twenty minutes. Serve very hot.

SAVARIN WITH STRAWBERRIES-MELBA

Dissolve one-fourth ounce compressed yeast in warm milk and make a paste with one-half pound flour. Add four eggs and mix well, cover and put in a warm place until dough has raised to double its size. Add six ounces of soft butter, a little salt and sugar and work thoroughly until very elastic. Fill in buttered savarin moulds and let rise. Bake in medium hot oven. When cold they are soaked in boiling syrup, flavor with lemon, orange, kirsch and cinnamon and place on dish; dress in center of the savarin some nice ripe strawberries and cover with raspberry syrup.

GENOISE CAKE

Four eggs and four ounces of sugar, powdered, are whisked over slow fire until very light, add vanilla flavoring and mix well but lightly with four ounces of flour and three ounces of melted butter. Bake in medium hot oven.

G. R. Meyer

LUCIEN FUSIER
CHEF DE CUISINE
GRAND HOTEL METROPOLE
Interlaken, Switzerland

Mr. Fusier was formerly at the Shepheard's Hotel at Cairo, the Grand Hotel du Louvre at Menton, France, Hotel Schweizerhof at Interlaken, Switzerland; Tunisia Palace, Tunis; the Yongfraublick Hotel at Interlaken, Switzerland, and at the Cap Hotel, Bordighera. Portugal.

MOUSSELINE CAKE

Beat eight yolks of eggs in a basin with a quarter of a pound of powdered sugar and a sprinkling of grated lemon. Mix therewith one-eighth pound of flour, one-eighth pound of melted butter and eight whites of eggs, duly beaten up. Cook this in a flat mould, then cut the biscuit horizontally in thin slices. Between two slices make a filling of cream of butter with kirsch, and fill the other slice with cream of butter put with chocolate. Glaze and decorate the cake with melted chocolate.

Lucien Fusier.

BRIOCHES

Work two ounces dissolved yeast, four ounces sifted flour and enough lukewarm milk to make a stiff sponge. Cover and set aside in warm place to rise.

Mix one and one-fourth pounds sifted flour and eight whole and six yolks of eggs, one and one-half pounds granulated sugar with one pound soft butter perfectly smooth. Beat the risen stiff sponge to the same and work the whole over. Set aside to rise to about twice its size. Place in refrigerator until firm. Work into round balls. Place in buttered moulds and a small ball on top. Let rise a little, mark them across with knife, wash with egg wash and bake in oven of about 425 degrees Fahrenheit for about twelve minutes. Serve warm for breakfast.

Charles A. Frey

CHAS. A. FREY
CHEF
HOTEL ALEXANDRIA
Los Angeles, Cal.

Mr. Frey was first at the Hotel von Konig von England in Munster; later at the Dom Hotel, Cologne; Continental Hotel, Paris; with the North German Lloyd and Hamburg-American Steamship Lines and Hotel Bellevue-Stratford, Philadelphia.

ADRIAN DELVAUX

CHEF DE CUISINE

HOTEL BALTIMORE

Kansas City, Mo.

Mr. Delvaux started in at the Grand Hotel in Rheims, France, and thence to the Bristol Hotel in Paris. In this country, at the Chicago Club, Hotel Congress and Annex, Chicago and at the Auditorium Hotel, Chicago. He has been at the Hotel Baltimore for five years, where he has made the Baltimore famous for its cuisine.

CORN MUFFINS

Take one-half pound of yellow corn meal, three-fourths pound soft wheat flour, two teaspoonfuls of baking powder, sift together in a bowl. Add to this five ounces of sugar, two eggs, four ounces melted butter, a pinch of salt; mix to a stiff batter and add one pint of milk. Have eight individual moulds, fill one-third full and put in hot oven and bake until done. Serve.

WAFFLES WITH RASPBERRY JAM

Take one pint of milk, two cups of flour, four tablespoonfuls of melted butter, two heaping teaspoonfuls of baking powder, a pinch of salt; mix thoroughly together and stir until very smooth. Then grease waffle irons and have them very hot. Pour batter in and allow them to stay until a crisp color. Serve with raspberry jam or any syrup or jelly desired.

HOME MADE RICE PUDDING

Boil one-half pound rice with water, put in a little cinnamon stick. When ready, strain and wash with cold water. Have ready made and cold, one pint of custard cream from the following ingredients: one pint milk, four yolks eggs, four ounces sugar, one ounce corn starch. Dissolve with the ready custard cream, then add one-half pint of sweetened whipped cream, and a pinch of salt. Fill up the pudding dishes and bake in a hot oven. When ready, sprinkle on top a little well flavored cinnamon sugar. Serve with plain cream on side.

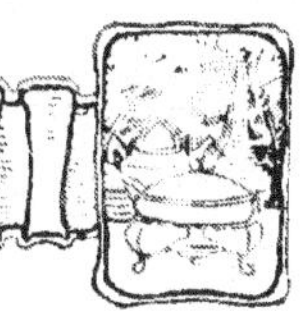

CAKE A LA ANNA

Yolks of four eggs beaten to the lightest possible cream, one cupful of sugar, pinch of salt, one and one-half teaspoonfuls of baking powder, sifted well with flour. Bake in two jelly cake pans.

Icing: Take the juice of a ripe pineapple, put some icing sugar in a vessel and incorporate the liquid slowly, just before using.

ERNEST OTZENBERGER
CHEF DE CUISINE
HOTEL DENNIS
Atlantic City, N.J.

Mr. Otzenberger was formerly Chef for G. W. Vanderbilt in Paris, London and New York.

CHERRY FRITTERS

Select one pound large and fine cherries, remove the pits and lay the fruit in a bowl. Sprinkle over with sugar, pour on a few spoonfuls of kirschwasser and let macerate for one hour. Then drain and thread eight of them on a silver skewer or a straw. Roll them in lady finger dust and dip in frying batter. Plunge them in hot frying fat and when the paste is fried and well cooked, drain off the fritters on a cloth, sponge them and dredge over with vanilla sugar, then dress in a pyramid on a folded napkin. Serve at the same time, a cherry sauce made with cherry juice and flavored with kirschwasser.

FRYING BATTER FOR SWEET DISHES

One-half pound flour, dilute it with tepid water, into which one ounce of butter has been melted, also salt. Make a soft very smooth batter, and when it has cooled off, add to it half a gill of brandy, two egg yolks, and two whites, beaten to a stiff froth.

Ernest Otzenberger

BEN E. DUPAQUIER

CHEF DE CUISINE

HOTEL ARLINGTON

Santa Barbara, Cal.

Mr. Dupaquier's first position was in The Pendennis Club, of Louisville, Ky. Later at the Gault House, Louisville, the Missouri Athletic Club, the Mercantile Club and the New Jefferson Hotel of St. Louis; the Jonathan Club and the California Club, Los Angeles and the Hotel Maryland, Pasadena, Cal.

FRENCH PANCAKE WITH JELLY

Four ounces sifted flour, half ounce powdered sugar, two whole raw eggs, one saltspoon salt, three-quarters pint good cold milk, eight drops vanilla essence, four drops orange flavoring and a tablespoonful Jamaica rum. Place the flour in a vessel, break in the eggs; add the sugar, salt, essences and the milk gradually. With a wire whisk briskly beat up the whole together for five minutes, or until thoroughly thickened. Then pass it through a Chinese strainer into another small vessel and let stand for thirty minutes. Have a tablespoonful melted butter on a saucer. Have a small frying pan, six inches in diameter at the bottom, lightly greased with the butter by means of a small hair pastry brush. When the bottom of the pan is thoroughly hot, pour the equivalent of three tablespoonfuls of the preparation into the pan and fry on a brisk fire until a nice golden color, which will take about a minute, then turn it over and fry exactly the same. Be very careful not to allow the cakes to get black. Carefully turn the cake on a hot plate on the corner of the range. Make eleven more in the same manner, lightly dredge with fine sugar on top, spread a thin layer on jelly, then roll the cakes up nicely and dredge just a little more sugar over them; lay on a hot dish and serve very hot.

PLUM PUDDING

Carefully remove the fibres and strings from a half pound of fresh beef kidney suet, chop finely with two tablespoonfuls flour and place in a large bowl, adding half a pound well picked and washed currants, half pound seeded Malaga grapes, quarter pound fresh bread crumbs, two ounces chopped candied lemon peel, half pound fine sugar, half teaspoonful ground cinnamon, one saltspoon ground nutmeg; half pint good rum and three eggs. Briskly mix the whole together with a wooden spoon for five minutes. Dip a piece of cloth in cold water and wring it out. Spread the cloth on a table, lightly butter with the hand and sprinkle a little flour over it; shake the cloth to remove the excess flour; place the contents of the bowl in the center of the cloth, bring up the four corners together so as to entirely enclose the pudding and lightly tie around. Have plenty of boiling water in a large pan and plunge in the pudding. Cover the pan and let it boil for two and a half hours. Remove it from the water and hang up for ten minutes. Cut the string and carefully turn it on a hot dish without breaking. Dredge with three tablespoonfuls of sugar, pour over one gill of rum, set it on fire and immediately serve with hard sauce separately.

HARD SAUCE

Place in a cool bowl one ounce good butter, two ounces fine sugar, half saltspoonful ground mace and five drops of vanilla essence. Set the bowl on broken ice and sharply beat up with a wooden spoon for five minutes, then keep in a cool place till required.

CORN MEAL MUFFINS

One-quarter pound wheat flour, one-half pound cornmeal, one-half ounce powdered sugar, one-half ounce good butter, one-half pint cold milk, one-half ounce baking powder, one-half teaspoonful salt and one whole raw egg. Place all these ingredients in a basin and carefully mix with the hand until thoroughly thickened, which will require about six minutes. Lightly butter the interior of six oval corn bread or muffin moulds. Place the preparation into the moulds up to three-quarters of their height. Lay them on a baking tin and bake in a hot oven for twenty minutes. Remove, dress on a hot dish with a folded napkin and serve.

Ben E. Dupaquier

HENRI BOUTROUE
CHEF DE CUISINE
HOTEL
SHELBOURNE
Dublin, Ireland

Mr. Boutroue was formerly with the Clifton Down Hotel at Bristol, England, the Queen's Hotel at Leeds, England, the Savoy Hotel in London; the Laugham, London, also the Hotel Metropole, London.

BLINIS

One-half ounce rye flour, one tablespoonful butter, mix with a quarter of a cup of milk, two eggs, one-half ounce melted butter. The mixture must have the consistency of freezing paste. Let rise to double its size, add two whites of eggs beaten and one-half pint of cream, and cook like pancakes.

Henri Boutroue

OLD FASHIONED BUCKWHEAT CAKES

Add to one pound of buckwheat flour one ounce of baking powder and a half teaspoonful of baking soda, mix with milk and water to a soft batter; add one-half cup of molasses, three ounces of melted butter, one-half ounce of salt and pour on hot griddle and bake as usual.

VIENNA BRIOCHES

Take one pint of milk, two ounces yeast one ounce sugar, pinch of salt, eight ounces butter and four eggs; make a light sponge with milk and yeast; when ready add the beaten eggs, sugar and salt, add the flour and last the butter. Make a medium dough; let come up and work over and set in a cool place for one hour to get firm; then form into different shapes twist, rolls, etc. Give good prove and bake in evenly heated oven to a nice brown.

John Bicochi

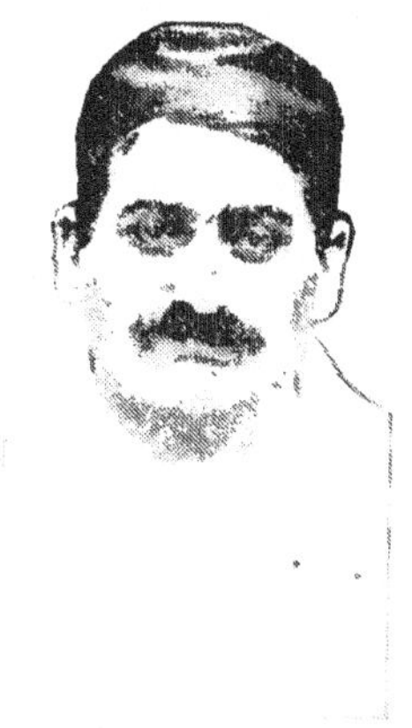

CHARLES
PIER GIORGI
CHEF DE CUISINE
HOTEL ALCAZAR
St. Augustine, Fla.

Prior to coming to the Hotel Alcazar, Mr. Giorgi was at the Hotel Walton and the Gilsey House, New York City; the Bay Shore House at City Island, N.Y.; the Hollywood Hotel at West End, N.J., and at the Hotel Kittatinny at Delaware Water Gap Pa.

WAFFLES

One quart flour, one pint milk, four teaspoonfuls baking powder, one teaspoonful salt, two tablespoonfuls melted butter and six eggs. Thoroughly beat the eggs for five minutes, add flour and baking powder, butter, salt and milk. Work good to a thin batter; heat waffle irons very hot, grease well with butter and fill with the batter and cook for five minutes. Serve immediately.

HONEY INDIAN SPOON BREAD

One quart water, two quarts milk, one-half pound cornmeal, one quarter pound honey, six eggs, one cup whipped cream, four ounces of butter, two teaspoonfuls baking powder, one teaspoonful of salt, three spoonfuls of powdered sugar.

Bring water and milk to a boil, add cornmeal, incorporate slowly with a whip, and let boil slowly for one-half hour. Separate the whites from the yolks of the eggs. Melt the honey and strain through cheesecloth and add to the cornmeal. Incorporate thoroughly and remove from the fire. Add the butter, the yolk of the eggs one at a time, keeping the whole well stirred. Add salt, sugar and baking powder. Beat the whites of the eggs to a froth add same to the whipped cream and stir lightly. Put the mixture in an earthen four quart bowl well buttered and bake in a slow oven for twenty minutes and serve immediately.

Chas Pier Giorgi

JULES BOUCHER
CHEF DE CUISINE
HOTEL ARLINGTON
Hot Springs, Ark.

Mr. Boucher served his apprenticeship at famous French Hotels and Cafes under Chefs world famous, such as Father Thiebout, of the Maison et Chabot of Paris, Chef Cassinin, of the Maisson Dorce, and was at the Restaurant Marguery, Palace Madelaine of Paris and the Cafe Royal of London. Coming to America he was at the Hotel Tourraine, Boston, Auditorium Hotel, Chicago, and the Detroit Club, at Detroit.

FRENCH PANCAKES AU CONFITURE
(Preserves)

Take a half pound of flour, salt, eight yolks of eggs, one pint of good rich milk, three ounces butter; make a batter; then add whites of eggs and mix the whole well and add, if you wish, vanilla or lemon. Take a few small frying pans and put in each a little clarified butter and cover the bottom of same with a very thin layer of the batter and when a nice golden brown is obtained, empty on the table and spread with preserves, jams or jellies. Roll them up, sprinkle with powdered sugar and burn with red hot poker.

J Boucher

PLUM PUDDING

Carefully remove the fibres and strings from a half pound fresh beef kidney suet, finely chop with little flour and place in a large bowl, adding currants, Malaga grapes, bread crumbs, chopped candied lemon peel, sugar, ground cinnamon, nutmeg, run and six eggs. Mix the whole all together for five minutes. Place the contents in a cloth, roll tightly and tie it around. Place pudding in steam for two and one-half hours. Place brandy over. Set on fire and serve.

Louis Thein

LOUIS THEIN
FORMERLY
CHEF DE CUISINE
HOTEL UTAH
Salt Lake City, Utah.

Mr. Thein has been with some of the best Hotels and Cafes in America.

JULES KOHLER
CHEF DE CUISINE
HOTEL ADLON
Berlin, Germany

Monsier Jules Kohler came to the Adlon from the most elegant and famous Restaurant in Paris, the "Cafe de Paris."

DELICES DE CAMEMBERT

(Camembert Delights)

Make eight small rolls of bun paste about one inch long. Split on side like eclair and fill with the following: One-half well cleaned camembert passed through a fine strainer, work over ice while adding one ounce butter and three or four spoonfuls of double cream until cheese becomes very light, add little salt and cayenne.

SOUFFLE AU CHESTER

(Chester Cheese Souffle)

Melt one-half pound butter, four ounces flour mixed in it, boil one pint of milk, pour over butter and flour and let cook a few minutes, then take off the stove and let cool. Add six yolks of eggs, two and one-half pounds grated chester cheese, salt and paprika. Beat whites of eight eggs and add to above mixture. Put in timbales, sprinkle grated Parmesan cheese over top and bake in moderate oven twenty minutes.

J. Kohler

QUEEN CAKES

Three ounces butter, four ounces sugar, work together in a bowl, add to it two eggs, one-half pint milk, work the whole and add two ounces currants, juice of one lemon, one table-spoonful of baking powder. Put the whole in baking pan and bake in moderate oven about twenty minutes. Cut in slices and serve hot.

J. Dauviller

PETER BONA
CHEF DE CUISINE
HOTEL CHAMBERLAIN
(Old Point Comfort)
Fortress Monroe, Va.

Mr. Bona's history since he arrived in this country is brief: three years at the Waldorf Astoria, New York City, in various capacities in the kitchen.

VIRGINIA BATTER BREAD

One-half pint water, ground meal (white meal), one-half teaspoonful salt, one teaspoonful baking powder, one-half tablespoon flour, one-half tablespoon of butter, one-half pint milk (sweet), two eggs; scald the meal in one-half pint of water. Heat the one-half pint milk and add to scalded meal and add the remainder of the ingredients, baking powder last, and stir well together. Divide this batter in two small pans and bake in a fast oven, about fifteen minutes. When batter is ready for baking it should be a little heavier than the consistency of milk. If same appears to be too thick add milk to reduce to proper consistency.

CORN CAKES

One-half pint white corn meal, unbolted, little salt, scald in very hot water, add one egg. Drop in small cakes about three inches in diameter and one-fourth inch thick, on a hot griddle and brown on both sides.

Peter Bona

A. SCHLOETTKE
CHEF DE CUISINE
WESTMINSTER HOTEL
Dresden, Germany

Mr. Schloettke served his apprenticeship at the Kalms Hotel at Brunswig, Germany. Since then he has served at the Traiteur Ferario, at Dresden, Germany; the Hotel Fahrhaus at Hamburg; the Dom Hotel at Cologne on Rhine; the Hotel Richmond at Geneva, Switzerland, the Hotel St. Croix, the Grand Hotel Bergeus, at Geneva, and the Grand Hotel du Parquis at Vevey, Switzerland.

PETITES SOUFFLES AU PARMESAN

Take about one-half ounce butter, same quantity of flour, add a cup of boiling milk, thicken with three yolks of eggs, and let cool. When cooled, mix one-half ounce of grated Parmesan cheese. Beat in the whites of eggs and empty the whole in timbales. Cook twenty minutes.

A. Schloettke

G. MILHAU
CHEF DE CUISINE
TAIT-ZINKAND CAFE
San Francisco, Cal.

Mr. Milhau learne his trade at the Ca Boudoul at Marseille France. Following th he was Chef at tl Grand Hotel De la Pa at Florence, Italy Coming to this countr he was at the Unic Club, Boston, the Tou raine Hotel, Boston, tl Metropolitan Club ar at the St. Regis Hot New York City. I came west with M Emile Bailly to open tl Fairmont Hotel in Sa Francisco.

TARTLETTES CALIFORNIA

Shape your moulds with short paste—then cook; put in a half of a peach and decorate around with cherries and strawberries. Cover the whole with a thick raspberry syrup flavored with maraschino.

G. Milhau

INTERNATIONAL COOKING LIBRARY

By the

World Famous Chefs

Complete in Ten Volumes

Vol. No. 1—**Salads and Salad Dressings**

" " 2—**Dainty Sweets** (Ices, Creams, Jellies and Preserves)

" " 3—**Ultra Select Dishes for Afternoon Teas**

" " 4—**Chafing Dish Specialties**

" " 5—**International Dessert and Pastry Specialties**

" " 6—**Bread and Pastry Recipes**

" " 7—**Soups and Consommes**

" " 8—**Fish, Oysters and Sea Foods**

" " 9—**Roasts and Entrees**

" " 10—**Relishes, Garnishings and Finishings**

EACH BOOK COMPLETE

This is undoubtedly the finest, most complete and most select set of books ever published in the culinary line. The special dishes of the World Famous Chefs, United States, Canada and Europe. Forty-seven contributors.

Price 50 cents per volume—NET

Sold by dealers everywhere or mail orders to

INTERNATIONAL PUBLISHING CO.

Los Angeles, Cal.

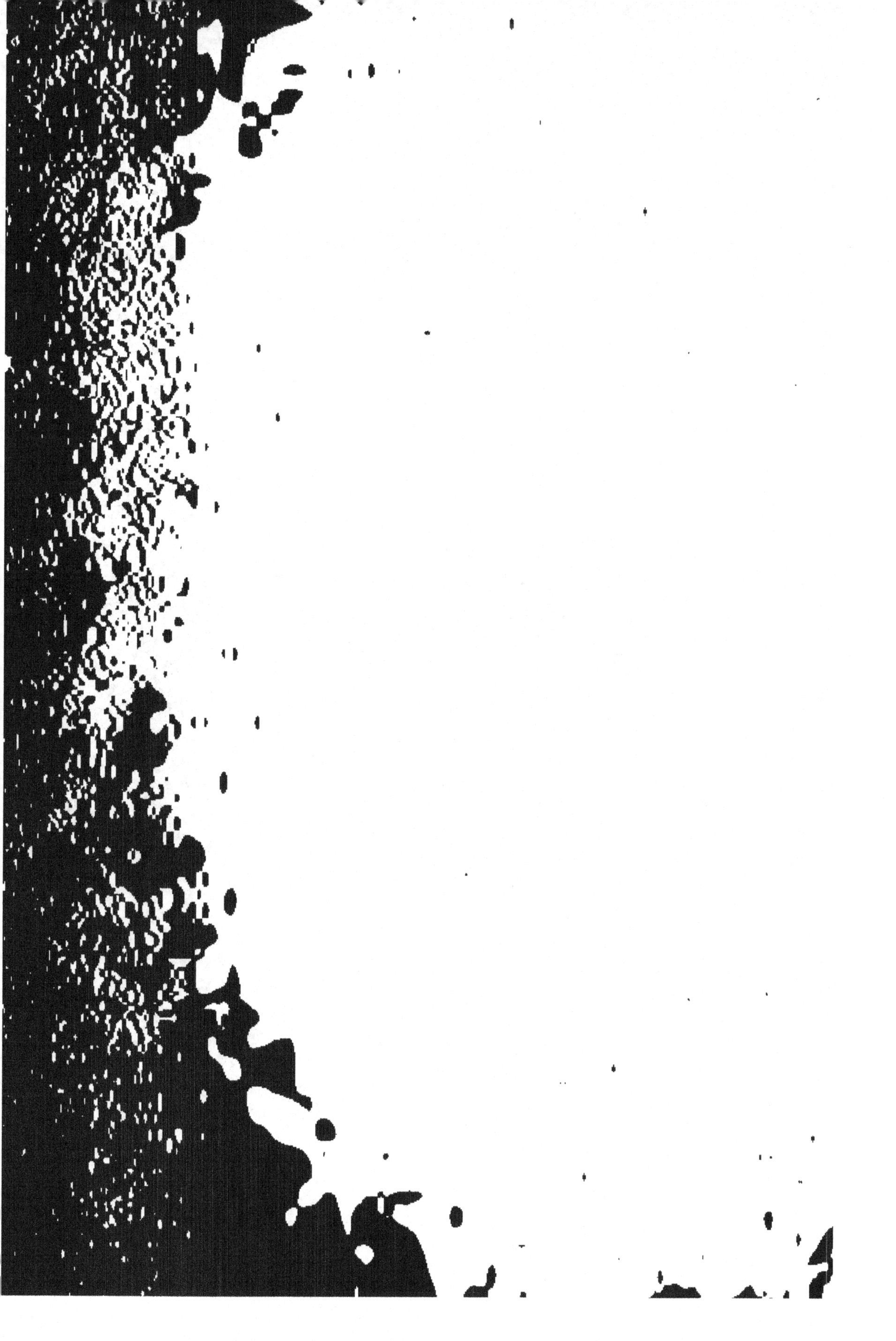

CPSIA information can be obtained
at www.ICGtesting.com
Printed in the USA
LVOW03s0848080216
474163LV00015B/434/P

9 781293 8161